"Lee Grady's book *Fearless Daughters of the Bible* provides powerful keys to help women unlock God's potential for their lives. The stories of biblical women and also modern-day women will encourage the reader to take bold steps of courage. It will help women close the door to past wound   equacies and old religious mind-sets. I high   aughters of the Bible* to all who   God!"

and president,
breakthrough Ministries

"In *Fearless Daught   ne Bible*, Lee Grady, who has championed the cause of women for many years, reveals the strengths and weaknesses of women God used throughout history. As you read Lee's insights into their lives, you'll find yourself. I did. This book is loaded with godly counsel to encourage and challenge us to unlock our self-imposed reservations and restrictions and release us to our destinies!"

Dr. Alice Smith, author/speaker;
executive director, U.S. Prayer Center

"J. Lee Grady's refreshing style brings to us this timely and timeless book that is an inspiration and a challenge to all women, redeemed by Christ and reclaimed as God's daughters. Come with Lee to the Scripture and discover the power and the purpose of women who dare to trust God."

LaDonna C. Osborn, D.Min.;
CEO, Osborn Ministries International;
president, Women's International Network;
bishop, International Gospel Fellowship of Churches & Ministries

"Lee Grady's *Fearless Daughters of the Bible* is a welcome effort to reclaim bold stories of godly women of the past. Their courageous actions raise the bar for this generation. I pray God will use this book to raise up fearless daughters for Him today."

Carolyn Custis James, author of *Half the Church*;
president, Whitby Forum

"It takes a fearless man to write a book like *Fearless Daughters of the Bible*. Lee Grady is such a man. After all, by his own admission, he has been 'drowning in a sea of estrogen for more than two decades. . . . For God put [him] in a house full of women to show [him] how much He loves His daughters.' I read the stories of the women in the book; now I must compile a list of men to whom I will send copies of *Fearless Daughters of the Bible* so they can see what a loving God really wants for His daughters."

Abby Olufeyimi, parish pastor, Builder's House (Redeemed
Christian Church of God), Croydon, England

Fearless Daughters of the Bible

What You Can Learn from
22 Women Who Challenged Tradition,
Fought Injustice and Dared to Lead

J. Lee Grady

Chosen
a division of Baker Publishing Group
www.ChosenBooks.com

© 2012 by J. Lee Grady

Published by Chosen Books
11400 Hampshire Avenue South
Bloomington, Minnesota 55438
www.chosenbooks.com

Chosen Books is a division of
Baker Publishing Group, Grand Rapids, Michigan

Printed in the United States of America

Library of Congress Cataloging-in-Publication Data is available for this title.

ISBN 978-0-8007-9531-3 (pbk.)

Unless otherwise indicated, Scripture quotations are from the New American Standard Bible®, copyright © 1960, 1962, 1963, 1968, 1971, 1972, 1973, 1975, 1977, 1995 by The Lockman Foundation. Used by permission.

Scripture quotations identified THE MESSAGE are from *The Message* by Eugene H. Peterson, copyright © 1993, 1994, 1995, 2000, 2001, 2002. Used by permission of NavPress Publishing Group. All rights reserved.

Scripture quotations identified KJV are from the King James Version of the Bible.

Cover design by Dan Pitts

12 13 14 15 16 17 18   7 6 5 4 3 2 1

To the fearless Christian women leaders I have worked with in 26 foreign countries during the past ten years. They include:

Funke Adejumo (Nigeria); Milagros Aguayo (Peru); Connie Birungi (Uganda); Sharon Bixler (Hungary); Monica Castro (Colombia); Emilia Ceuta (Romania); Aida Cornejo (Ecuador); Athena D'Souza (Singapore); Mercedes Dalton (El Salvador); Naomi Dowdy (Singapore); Yinka Ekwugum (Nigeria); Eunice Enujuba (Nigeria); Indri Gautama (Indonesia); Lilla Gere (Hungary); Dellis Gomes (India); Teresa Gomez (Peru); Carol Hanes (Australia); Royree Jenson (Australia); Doreen Kaahwa (Uganda); Angela Kovacs (Hungary); Gloria Madugba (Nigeria); Judy Mbugua (Kenya); Nori Menendez (Colombia); Esther Milian (Colombia); Ilma Morales (Guatemala); Mihaela Moza (Romania); Eva Nagy (Hungary); Remi Ogunrinde (Canada); Deola Ojo (Nigeria); Abby Olufeyimi (England); Hala Saad (Egypt); Silvia Comacho Salcedo (Bolivia); Natalia Schedrivaya (Russia); Igna Suarez (Colombia); Mariamma Thampy (India); Taiwo Thompson (Nigeria); Ingrid Tressler (South Africa); Ansa van Neikerk (South Africa); Rodica Voluntiru (Canada); Daphne Yang (Singapore); and Bini Zachariah (India)

These brave women proved to me that God is serious about raising up an army of gifted, empowered women leaders in the Church today. They are models of sacrifice, character, humility and radical devotion to Christ.

Contents

Contents

Foreword

Throughout the years I've spent writing and teaching, I've found godly men who have been not only gatekeepers but champions of women using all the gifts that God has given them. And I'm grateful for every single one. Their kind words, generous encouragement and gracious support have meant more than they will ever know.

While some may wonder why a man would write a book about women, I don't ask such questions. Instead, I simply say thank-you.

Thank you, Lee Grady, for reminding us that God's fearless daughters line the pages of the Bible. Each of their stories serves as a courageous call to follow God with abandon—serving, loving, leading and leaning into all that God has for each one of us.

Throughout the upcoming pages, you're going to hear stories of much-beloved as well as lesser-known women found in Scripture. Audacious faith, bold prayers and a passionate love for God mark their adventures. Each of these biblical stories is complemented by more modern examples of women from around the globe who are living courageous lives—introducing people to Christ, helping free people from the entrapment of sin and transforming communities.

Through vivid storytelling, we are reminded that the stories of *Fearless Daughters of the Bible* are meant to be all our stories. We're called and created to be a people who pursue God with everything we've been given—all for the glory of God.

My hope and prayer is that through the upcoming pages you'll sense the areas in your own life where God is calling you to become more courageous. And along the way you'll find yourself looking and acting even more like your heavenly Father.

Margaret Feinberg
Author of *Scouting the Divine* and *The Sacred Echo*
www.margaretfeinberg.com

Introduction

Reclaiming Your Father's Love

You may wonder why a guy is writing a book for women. I am asked that question often since I speak at women's events all over the world. I respond by telling people that I have been drowning in a sea of estrogen for more than two decades. God put me in a house full of women to show me how much He loves His daughters.

1985 was the year my wife, Deborah, and I had our first baby—a girl we named Margaret. Less than two years later we had our second baby, another girl, Meredith. Almost two years later we had a third girl, Gloria. (We had multiple girls in disposable diapers at one time, and we probably have a landfill somewhere with the Grady name on it.) Three years after Gloria's arrival we made room for Charlotte, our fourth daughter. Four girls in fewer than seven years!

I was in the delivery room for each birth, but I cannot say I did too much to help except stroke my wife's arm, offer reassuring comments and stay out of the nurse's way. I felt helpless while my wife strained, sweated, gasped and pushed. Birth is an awful, painful, bloody mess—and quite humbling for a father who feels responsible for the pain yet cannot do a thing to alleviate it except pace the hospital floor.

In all but one case we knew we were having a girl because of an ultrasound image (Meredith crossed her legs for the picture to keep us guessing). But I can promise you that I never once felt a tinge of disappointment when I learned I would be the father of a daughter. I was overjoyed each time.

I will never forget when Margaret finally emerged from the birth canal around 7 A.M., all slimy and shivering at her first contact with outside air. I burst into tears as soon as I heard her pitiful, whimpering cry. I was in awe as I studied her tiny feet, the cleft in her chin and the way the skin on her fingers had wrinkled in the amniotic fluid.

The reality hit me hard: I was a father, and this precious little girl was mine to raise. I felt this same ecstatic joy when each of my daughters was born. I never thought, *I wish I could have a boy*, or, *Why does God keep giving me girls?* In fact, after our second was born, I figured we might as well keep the girls coming. (*We're on a roll! Let's have a matched set!*) And as my girls grew up, they knew Daddy celebrated them.

I certainly will not pretend I was the perfect father. All dads have regrets—about business trips we should have canceled, vacations we should have planned or harsh words we wish we had never said. But as I look back on our family life, I can say I gave my girls a gift many people in the world today have never known: a loving, affirming environment in which to thrive.

You can imagine that life in the Grady household was infused with feminine energy. There were Barbie dolls, baby dolls, china dolls, cupcake dolls, dollhouses and an Anne of Green Gables doll that never left the top bookshelf because it looked expensive. There were stuffed animals of every genus and species. There were crayons, watercolor paints, glitter paint, glitter pens, sidewalk chalk and chalkboards. There were drawers full of hair bands, hair ties and barrettes of every size and color. There were roller skates, inline skates, tricycles, bicycles, jump ropes and Hula-Hoops. And there were shoes. So many shoes!

When the girls grew old enough to enjoy movies, our house became the second home for Pocahontas, the Swan Princess, Cinderella, Sleeping Beauty, Mulan, the Little Mermaid and Belle from *Beauty and the Beast*. By the time they were preteens, we probably had the largest collection of estrogen-laced entertainment in Florida. This included a movie we all related to in some strange way: *Little Women*, the story of how four daughters grew up, discovered romance and struggled to find value in a male-dominated world. (I was not fond of the fact that the father in Louisa May Alcott's story was wounded while fighting in the Civil War.)

When my daughters entered their teen years, the estrogen level increased tenfold—and I felt as if I were the victim of a home invasion. These cute, obedient children turned into moody women with attitudes. Like all girls their age, they pouted, cried, fought with each other (most often over sharing clothes), rolled their eyes, questioned my authority, tested my wife's patience and broke a few boys' hearts.

It was also during these teen years that my daughters' bathroom (yes, they shared the same one) became a veritable warehouse of feminine products including lipstick, mascara, eye shadow, eyebrow pencils, eyebrow tweezers, foundation, face powder, acne medicine, fingernail polish, fingernail polish remover, fingernail files, hair gel, hair mousse, hair spray, glitter lotion, body lotion, body spray, feminine napkins (which we purchased in bulk quantities), face wash, clay masks, blackhead remover, triple-action astringent, disposable razors (always in pink) and something called cream bleach—which, I learned from my daughters, is the best way for a girl to remove any trace of a moustache. (The first time I found this substance in their bathroom, along with measuring spoons and a bowl from the kitchen, I thought one of the girls was conducting a chemistry experiment.)

All of these products, along with various items of clothing, could be found on any given day in any location in our four-bedroom house. And because I was the only male in our home (apart from our dachshund, Flapjack), and I was so ignorant of the ways and means of females, I was usually the first suspect when anything went missing. If I found a tube of lip gloss on the floor, for example, my tendency was to throw it away since I assumed it was empty. My girls trained me always to ask before discarding anything—no matter how much it looked like garbage.

Once I noticed a suspicious curved wire on our kitchen counter, and my temptation was to put it in the trash immediately. But because I had been trained properly, I resisted the impulse to discard it and waited to consult my wife. "What is this?" I asked her when she came home from the store. Drawing from her vast maternal wisdom, she replied: "Oh, that's the wire from one of the girls' bras. It fell out in the dryer. Don't throw it away."

Dad scored a point! I did not throw away the bra wire! I was learning how to survive in this complex world of women. It is true that I did get my first gray hairs during this season of life (especially when I was teaching my oldest girls to drive), but overall the experience of raising a family in this hormone-rich environment was as personally rewarding as it was unforgettable. I have absolutely loved being a dad of girls.

What Does "Father" Mean to You?

I figured out early in my parenting days that children need affection and encouragement along with discipline. Even though I faced a lot of financial pressure to feed, clothe and house our big family, I tried to invest as much time as possible in their formation. That meant lots of laughter around our dinner table, story times at night (they especially liked it when I made up adventures about an imaginary dog), games (one of their favorites was acting out our own version of *Jurassic Park*—and I was the velociraptor), birthday trips to Disney World, Sea World or the zoo, after-hours visits to my office (where they could ride an elevator) and many, many birthday parties.

We also had what I called "Daddy days" when my wife needed to shop, visit a friend or attend a church function. On those days, it was my turn to change diapers, make sandwiches, fill cups with juice, wipe up spills, comb the girls' hair ("Dad, that hurts!") and—most importantly—coordinate playtimes. I tried to be creative, but usually I let my girls direct our activities. These ranged from stuffed animal parades (we had enough dogs, cats, lions, otters and bears to march from the back bedroom to the front of the house) to hikes in the woods to elaborate reenactments of *Star Wars* or *The Wilderness Family*.

When my girls were small I did not consciously strategize to pour affection on them in order to build their confidence. I was not that smart. Somehow most of this came intuitively; it is just what fathers do. I hugged and cuddled them. I prayed for them at night. I bought them little surprises at the store and brought home gifts from business trips. I tried to shower them with love. When my girls were almost grown, I began to realize they had developed impressive confidence.

Margaret, my oldest, got involved in our church's youth group and began to show leadership qualities. She ended up serving in student government in high school and going on church mission trips. When she came home from her first overseas adventure—to the Dominican Republic—she stood in front of the congregation and described the poverty she saw on that island nation. Through tears she told the crowd: "I will never complain again that my family only has two bathrooms!"

Our second daughter was quite shy when she was young—so shy that she was afraid of talking on the telephone. But by the time she had reached eleventh grade she landed the starring role in the Tony Award–winning play *Proof* and became known in high school as a gifted actress. By the time she got to college she was writing plays as well as hard-hitting editorials and blogs.

Gloria, our third daughter, led her high school's dance troupe during football games and helped lead worship in her youth group. During her college years she spent her summers on the mission field, serving orphans in India and teaching English to children in Rwanda.

Our youngest, Charlotte, discovered her own acting talents in middle school and excelled on stage in high school. Whether she was playing the role of the nurse in *Romeo and Juliet* or the lead role in *A Midsummer Night's Dream*, she exuded confidence on and off the stage.

I certainly will not take credit for my girls' accomplishments. Every person is born with God-given talents. But I do believe that a loving environment—and a healthy home life—is the key to building a healthy self-image. This is especially important for girls, who grow up in a culture in which they are demeaned as sex objects or dismissed as second-class citizens, even in church.

I will never forget when I took Margaret to enroll in college in Georgia in 2004. It was an emotional moment for me and my wife as we loaded up our car with her clothes, books, pillows and bedspreads. I was taking my firstborn child—the precocious girl who learned to wrap me around her little finger—to a campus nine hours from home. Just as we were about to pull out of the driveway I spotted something unusual in the backseat: a stack of posters that said MARGARET GRADY FOR STUDENT GOVERNMENT.

When I asked about this, Margaret shared with me her plan to influence Emmanuel College. ("One of these days," she told me later of the school, "I'd like to help run this place.") When we arrived on the Emmanuel campus and pulled in front of Jackson Hall, the girls' dormitory, a young man who was a sophomore on campus offered to help move boxes to Margaret's room. On his third or fourth trip to the car he saw the posters and stared at them for a few moments. He scratched his head and looked at me with disbelief.

"What kind of a girl comes to campus as a freshman and already has designed her political posters?" he asked. I just laughed. Then I pondered his question. *What kind of girl is this?* I thought. The answer: *A confident girl.*

Many women (and a lot of men, too) struggle with self-image issues because of what I call "the father wound." Whether we like it or not, our parents play a huge role in shaping our core identity and character. If our moms and dads showered us with love, we have a healthy view of ourselves and find it easy to thrive. But if our fathers or mothers were dysfunctional, we end up being dysfunctional as well.

Let me ask you: What do you feel emotionally when I mention the word *father*? Do you have warm thoughts of security, provision and affection? Does the word conjure up thoughts of love and appreciation? Or does it strike a painful chord? Does it trigger feelings of anxiety, frustration, anger or bitterness? Or does the word *father* make you feel numb and cold?

17

Over the past ten years I have ministered to hundreds of women and men who struggle because of poor parenting. Through my experience I have identified six types of dysfunctional fathers. Perhaps you know one of these:

1. *The absent father.* This is the dad who was never there. He may have died (and children sometimes blame a parent for dying, even though this is irrational). Or, the father may have abandoned the mother after she had her child—or perhaps he was never home at all. Whatever the case, an absentee father creates a huge gap for a child who needs paternal approval.

2. *The distant father.* This is the father who was physically in the home but was disengaged. He may have been depressed. Or maybe he never learned to show emotion because of painful experiences in his own life such as post-traumatic stress disorder or physical abuse. This type of dad finds it very difficult to show affection to a child or to say, "I love you." So the child, who is starved for healthy affection, will assume that he or she is not loved.

3. *The critical father.* Many children grow up to hate their fathers (or mothers) because of negativity in the home. While parents must discipline their children in order to steer them in the right moral direction, a father who constantly berates his son or daughter will severely impair that child's success. This type of parent is often found in legalistic religious homes. Strict discipline imposed without a demonstration of tender love can turn a child away from faith.

4. *The addicted father.* Some people grow up with dads who are alcoholics or drug addicts. In these cases, a child does not know who his father is. One day he is fun to be with, the next day he is a monster. One day he is playful and friendly,

18

the next day he has red eyes and a frightening demeanor. This can traumatize a child who needs to feel secure at home. Children of alcoholics face severe struggles later in life because they do not know whom to trust—especially if their own fathers were out of control.

5. *The abusive father.* A large percentage of women today have experienced some level of abuse—physical, verbal or sexual. In one country where I minister regularly, Peru, up to 30 percent of the women in some areas say they were sexually abused by their own fathers. (Among indigenous communities in Peru, this often happens because families sleep in the same bed, and incest becomes an ugly secret that is never addressed.)

A woman who has been abused by her own father will often plunge into deep depression later in life—mainly because she is not allowed to talk about the shame she carries. She is forced to bury all memory of the crime, and the wound begins to fester. Abused women tend to blame themselves for the sin, even though they hated what happened to them and did nothing to instigate it. Also, some girls who are abused are told that something terrible will happen to them if they ever report the incident.

6. *The passive father.* While a critical father is harsh and demanding, a passive father is at the other end of the spectrum. He may be in the house every day, but he never offers his children advice, counsel or correction. This might be because he has a long-term illness or a serious emotional problem. But even some otherwise healthy fathers find themselves incapable of providing the protective discipline a child needs. Psychologists have proven that children feel more protected when they are given boundaries. If they are allowed to run

wild, they become nervous, insecure and fearful, as well as rowdy and erratic. (Later, when they enter the teen years, they can develop serious rebellion and immoral behavior patterns.) God designed us with a need for moral limitations, and parents have a responsibility to provide this through loving discipline.

You might feel tempted to be depressed after reading this list—especially if I described your dad in one or more of the paragraphs above. You may have even buried painful memories of your father's behavior. But I want to encourage you: You are not stuck in a place of pain. Your heavenly Father wants to heal any and every hurt you experienced during your upbringing.

Your healing begins with this passage from 1 John 3:1:

> See how great a love the Father has bestowed on us, that we would be called children of God; and such we are. For this reason the world does not know us, because it did not know Him.

The disciple John, who penned these words as well as the gospel that bears his name, used the word *father* almost 150 times in his New Testament writings. He, more than any other follower of Christ, understood that God is our Father and that Jesus was in perfect unity with the Father. And in the above passage he tells us that we must "see" how great the Father's love is toward us. The Father's love is a revelation!

Do you truly believe the Father loves you? If we have struggled in life with fathers who were addictive, abusive, absent or critical, the very word *father* can be revolting. So when someone mentions that God is our Father, we can project our earthly fathers' mistakes and flaws onto God. And this will seriously hinder our relationship with Him.

It is important to remember that God is a perfect Father; He will never make the mistakes your earthly father or mother made. This means:

- Even though your earthly father may have been absent from the home, God has promised that He "will not fail you or forsake you" (Joshua 1:5). He is always there. He is "a very present help in trouble" (Psalm 46:1). He will never abandon you.

- Though your father may have been distant, and never showed any affection for you, our heavenly Father is full of mercy and compassion. He is so loving, in fact, that He draws His wayward children back to Himself—even when they rebel. Like the father in the story of the Prodigal Son, our heavenly Father runs after us, embraces us and kisses us when we decide to return to Him. God is full of affection!

- While your earthly father may have been critical, judgmental or harsh in his discipline, it is not so with God. Our heavenly Father is kind and gracious, and He is willing to forgive our mistakes instantly when we are honest about them. He even chooses to forget our sins. He does not keep a record of wrongs.

- Even though your earthly father may have been addicted to drugs, alcohol or gambling, God's character is unchanging. He does not act one way today and another way tomorrow. He is "the same yesterday and today and forever" (Hebrews 13:8). He never gets drunk, high or out of control. We can trust Him when all else fails. He is unshakable and forever faithful.

- If your father was abusive in any way, you must realize that God never abuses people. God hates abuse. It was not God's will for you to be hurt in this way; abuse is the result of the sinful choices of human beings who forsake the love of God.

- While your earthly father might have been passive and lenient—as if he did not really care what happened to you—your heavenly Father watches over you with tender care. He is willing to intervene if necessary to rescue you from your own hurtful actions, and He disciplines us in mercy to correct and protect us. God's discipline is perfect.

If you had a loving father or stepfather while growing up, you are blessed. But if you struggled in a home with a dysfunctional father, you can be healed completely. God can fill in every gap with His great love. If you feel unloved, choose to receive the Father's affection; if you feel insecure, run into His strong arms; if you feel depressed because of abuse, remember that your heavenly Father was grieved when you were violated. And He can restore your broken heart.

As we begin this study of the most confident women in the Bible—women who faced all kinds of difficulties in life—open your heart to receive a full revelation of the love of the Father. You may struggle with depression, self-hatred, resentment, disappointment, shame, fear or anxiety—but God can free you from every bondage and transform you into a confident, joyful, fearless woman. Put on your seat belt and prepare for an incredible journey toward total restoration.

The questions for women at the end of each chapter are designed for either individual use or small group discussion. You are also encouraged to read prayerfully "A Message from Your Heavenly Father."

————— Let's Talk about It —————

1. Recall a time when you received affirmation from your father that made a positive impression on you. What did he say, and why was it so meaningful?

2. Read over the list of fathers starting on page 18. Do any of these describe your father? In what ways did your parents shape the woman you are today?
3. Love from a father and mother can build healthy confidence and security in a child. How would you describe your confidence level today? Is it low, high or somewhere in between? Why?
4. If you had more confidence, what would you like to accomplish in life that you have been afraid of attempting? Share your dreams with someone close to you or those in your group.

A MESSAGE FROM YOUR HEAVENLY FATHER

My precious daughter,

I rejoiced the day you were born. You are very special to Me! Zephaniah 3:17 says that I rejoice over you "with shouts of joy"! I went to extravagant lengths to make you the way you are. When I formed you in your mother's womb, it took 113 billion miles of DNA strands to describe all your unique characteristics. You are unique in every way, not just in physical qualities but in all the special personality traits I gave you.

Don't ever doubt My love. Even though at times people will disappoint you, I will always be steadfast and constant in My love for you. People may reject, abandon, betray, abuse, devalue, ignore or criticize you, but their actions don't reflect how I feel about you.

Don't allow what people have said or done to you to distort the way you view Me. I am Your Father, and I am full of mercy and compassion. I will never leave you. I will never abuse you. And even when I discipline you, I do it out of love so you can learn My ways and grow up to be the daughter I created you to be—a daughter who looks and acts like her Father.

1

Sarah, the Mother of Our Faith

The Courage to Be a Pioneer

God intended women to be outside as well as
men, and they do not know what they are missing
when they stay cooped up in the house.

—Annie Oakley (1860–1926),
American sharpshooter and
women's rights advocate

When the New World was being discovered in the 1400s and 1500s, all the celebrated explorers who circumnavigated the globe were European males. Christopher Columbus, Vasco da Gama, Hernando De Soto, Ferdinand Magellan and Juan Ponce de León were just a few of the brave men who opened up trade routes and proved the world was round. They were the heroes of the day.

Meanwhile, the women of that time period didn't get out much. Most of them worked in the fields from an early age (although they were paid much less than men), they spent a lot of time sewing or milking cows, and they were not allowed to join trade guilds. Once they were married they were under the strict control of their husbands, and about 20 percent of women in medieval times died in childbirth.[1]

Yet if you dig deeper into history you find that women, even though they faced serious disadvantages, have also been pioneers. One example is Margaret Heffernan Borland, an Irish immigrant to the United States who was this nation's first cattle rancher. She overcame incredible odds on the prairie: After her first husband died in a gun battle, and her second husband died of cholera, she married a wealthy rancher—who then died of yellow fever. The disease killed several of Margaret's children and she became the sole owner of her ranch. In 1873 she drove her own herd of ten thousand cattle up the Chisholm Trail to reach Wichita, Kansas.[2] Her resourceful life exemplifies the brave pioneer spirit that was so evident in the founding of America.

Many women throughout history have been pioneers. Florence Nightingale founded the modern profession of nursing, and she bravely led a group of nurses to Crimea to care for war victims at a time when women were not welcome on the battlefield. Marie Curie, who developed modern radiology, was the first woman and the first scientist to receive a Nobel Prize. Patricia Bath was the first African American woman to receive a patent for a medical invention (she developed a laser device to remove cataracts). In 1963, a Russian woman, Valentina Tereshkova, became the first woman cosmonaut. She orbited the earth for three days, and today an asteroid and a crater on the moon are named in her honor.

When you read the Bible it is obvious that God often anoints women to be initiators. He did not create women just to follow the guys around. In fact, when He decided to send His only begotten

Son into the world, He looked for a woman. He sent an angel to a virgin named Mary in Nazareth, and He did not ask her father's permission or seek her fiancé's approval before causing her to become supernaturally impregnated with the divine seed. God sought out a woman to do this miracle. He challenged the norms of culture and broke with patriarchal tradition.

He did the same when He called Sarah, the wife of Abraham, to be the mother of our faith. Isaiah 51:1–2 tells all of us, both men and women, to look to Sarah as a role model:

> "Listen to me, all you who are serious about right living and committed to seeking God. Ponder the rock from which you were cut, the quarry from which you were dug. Yes, ponder Abraham, your father, and Sarah, who bore you. Think of it! One solitary man when I called him, but once I blessed him, he multiplied."
>
> THE MESSAGE

Sarah was chosen for a starring role in God's redemptive plan, but it was not because of her qualifications or pedigree. We are told she was beautiful (and her movie-star beauty actually got her into trouble a few times), but beauty could not help her overcome her most serious physical limitation. If you or I had gone searching for a candidate to be the mother of a nation, we certainly would not have picked an infertile woman. We would have left this young bride in Ur.

When we first meet Sarah (known as Sarai at that time), Genesis 11:30 describes her in painfully blunt terms: "Sarai was barren; she had no child." She and her husband, Abram, left their comfortable surroundings and went on a search for the Promised Land after the true God made an outlandish promise to them: "I will make you a great nation" (Genesis 12:2).

It is actually a pitiful scene—much like when Jed Clampett, Jethro, Elly May and Granny headed to California in their rickety truck in *The Beverly Hillbillies*. In the case of Abram and Sarai, the God of the universe interrupted life in a pagan culture and called this man and his wife to leave their idolatry. In obedience they saddled up their donkeys, loaded up their caravan with their possessions and a few straggling relatives and began to head west.

They had no map, no clear destination and no guarantee of a home once they got to Canaan. They became nomads, searching in the dark for a divine promise and trusting their new God with every step. Abram "went out, not knowing where he was going" (Hebrews 11:8), and he did not drag his wife behind him by the hair like an Iron Age Neanderthal. Sarai was with him all the way. All they had to guide them was an elusive promise from a God who had only recently introduced Himself to them. And this God kept telling Abram: "To your descendants I will give this land" (Genesis 12:7).

What was going on in Sarai's mind when this motley crew pulled out of Ur to begin their epic journey? Did she think Abram was crazy? Did she protest the move? Or did she immediately latch on to the promise of a child and load a crib onto one of the camels?

The Bible does not give us too many details, nor does it show us how this mother of Israel processed the promise through so many tests and trials. All we know is that throughout her trek across the ancient Mesopotamian wilderness, she became a worshiper of this amazing God. During the journey, the Lord repeated His original promise seven times—and both Abram and Sarai came to believe that He could do the impossible.

They trusted Him together. Their faith grew stronger. They held on to their promise even into old age, and in the end their faith became the necessary channel for God's miracle. They became role models of what it means to believe. And they set the stage for this amazing God to create the Jewish nation, and eventually to send His promised Savior into the world.

Go West, Young Woman

I have met some impressive pioneering women during my travels. One is Naomi Dowdy, who began her journey in her twenties when she left her home in Southern California and moved to the tiny Marshall Islands to be a missionary with the Assemblies of God. She had no husband and no money, but she led people to Christ and served small churches in that Pacific island culture for several years.

Then she was offered an unusual job: Church officials asked her to become senior pastor of a small congregation in the Asian nation of Singapore. Naomi resisted. Even though her denomination ordained women and sometimes set them in pastoral office, she was not eager to fight cultural stereotypes and deal with the criticism she knew would come her way. But when she prayed about it, God told her to take the position. She felt she had no choice but to submit to God's plan.

Thirty years after Naomi said yes to this assignment, Trinity Christian Centre had grown to become one of the largest churches in Singapore, with more than 6,500 members in 2012. She developed a small group model that is now duplicated in churches around the world, and the man she trained to be her replacement, Dominic Yeo, became the leader of the Assemblies of God in his nation. Once when I visited Trinity shortly after Naomi handed over her pastoral duties to her successor, members of the church pledged more than $9 million (U.S.) to invest in overseas missions. It has become a powerful influence throughout Asia.

Naomi never married and she has no natural children. But having invested most of her life in the mission field, she has produced more spiritual children than she can count. With each step of faith, even those awkward baby steps in the earliest years, she created a legacy that now benefits countless thousands of people on several continents. This is how faith works. It starts small, but in the end it grows huge. The mustard seed becomes a giant tree that gives shade to many.

Whenever God wants to do something in the earth, He always looks for a man or a woman to work through. He does not look for the rich or the qualified, or for those who are confident in their own abilities. He looks for someone who will step out of the way and allow God to work through him. He looks for someone who will lift her hands in surrender and say the words of the prophet Isaiah: "Here am I. Send me!" (Isaiah 6:8). He wants a person who is willing to volunteer to be a pioneer.

God can use you in this way, and when you surrender He will take you on a journey of faith just as He did Sarai. It will have plenty of bumps and jolts; it may be scary at times; it will not come without a cost. Pioneers never have it comfortable—but they receive the best rewards. Are you willing to walk on this less inviting path?

Sarai and her husband had many ups and downs in their walk with the Lord. In the first half of their story, Abram lied to Pharaoh about Sarai's identity and narrowly avoided a tragedy. Sarai struggled with doubt. Even though God continually promised He would give Abram and Sarai their own biological son, she convinced her husband to sleep with her maid, Hagar, in order to produce an heir—and that idea ended up in a complicated mess that had notorious repercussions for generations.

Yet the Bible tells us that after the fiasco with Hagar and her baby, Ishmael, God repeated His promise again to Abram: "I have made you the father of a multitude of nations" (Genesis 17:5). God also told His chosen servant that He would change his name. He said in the same verse: "No longer shall your name be called Abram, but your name shall be Abraham." God also said He wanted to change Sarai's name. Genesis 17:15–16 says:

Then God said to Abraham, "As for Sarai your wife, you shall not call her name Sarai, but Sarah shall be her name. I will bless her, and indeed I will give you a son by her. Then I will bless her, and she shall be a mother of nations; kings of peoples will come from her."

Why was the name change so important? The shift from Abram ("exalted father") to Abraham ("father of a multitude") is obvious. Sarai ("princess") is changed to Sarah ("princess of nations") indicating increased authority and influence. God blessed both of His chosen servants with these new names to proclaim His special destiny over them.

Bible scholars including Matthew Henry have also pointed out that this unique name change involved the insertion of the Hebrew *H* "breath" sound—which is part of the name of God—Yahweh or YHWH (which is rendered "Lord" and derived from the verb "to be").[3] The renaming of Abraham and Sarah shows that God was willing to pull them close to Himself in intimate relationship, and to give them His very name. They became more closely identified with Him by being drawn into a covenant relationship. They took His name as their own.

This is what happens to us when we give our hearts to Jesus Christ and receive the gift of salvation. We receive a new name because we are baptized "into Christ" (Romans 6:3), and when we are in Christ all things become new (see 2 Corinthians 5:17). We enter a covenant relationship with God that is like a marriage bond, and He pledges His loyalty. He promises to be with us forever. Suddenly our limitations fall away as we receive our measure of faith. The indwelling Christ gives us courage to believe and to become "more than conquerors" (Romans 8:37, KJV). We can now do all things through Christ.

Because Sarah lived before the coming of Jesus, she did not experience the new birth as we know it. But she was a prototype of New Covenant faith. Her transformation from Sarai to Sarah tells us that anything is possible when God joins with us in intimate fellowship. When you are connected to Him, everything changes. Your barrenness is transformed into fruitfulness and your emptiness is filled with hope.

It was not long after Sarah's name change that the Lord visited Abraham and Sarah in their tent by the oaks of Mamre. Sarah was old by this time, and past childbearing years, but in Genesis 18:14 the Lord restated His promise and said, "Is anything too difficult for the LORD? At the appointed time I will return to you, at this time next year, and Sarah will have a son."

At first Sarah laughed when she heard this declaration. How could her dry womb function properly? How could her 99-year-old husband become a father? All the laws of nature said God was lying. But after a few more faith struggles the prophecy proved true. Genesis 21:1–2 says:

> Then the LORD took note of Sarah as He had said, and the LORD did for Sarah as He had promised. So Sarah conceived and bore a son to Abraham in his old age, at the appointed time of which God had spoken to him.

Sarah had her own vibrant relationship with God. She was not just being dragged around in the desert with camels, donkeys and handmaidens to serve Abraham's God. She was not just a spectator in this drama. She had a key role, and God could not have achieved His goals without her. She proves that God has always—even from the book of Genesis—planned to involve women in His redemption plan.

Many Christian women today feel marginalized, even in church, by sexist or patriarchal attitudes. Some are allowed no other service in church except to teach children, prepare food for church functions, attend prayer meetings or lead women's Bible studies. In some traditional Christian environments we are led to believe that women in the Bible were like members of a Greek chorus who stood in the shadows and cheered as the men did all the important work.

That is not the message of Scripture. God calls women to know Him. He wants a close, personal, intimate relationship with His daughters—so close that He pulls them into the center of His plans. He wants to use them. He draws them into a covenant relationship with Him, gives them His name and empowers them to be spiritual pioneers.

Equal Partners in Faith

Abraham and Sarah are models to us of biblical partnership between the sexes. We see this pattern first demonstrated in the Garden of Eden, where God created human beings and called them to rule over the earth. When He formed mankind, the Bible says He created them male and female in His own image (see Genesis 1:26–27). This means that God's divine character and attributes cannot be seen in only one sex; it takes men and women together to reflect God's divine nature.

When God created the mountains, the trees, the clouds and the birds—everything in nature—He always said, "It is good." But when He made the man, He did not say that. Notice what He declared in Genesis 2:18: "Then the LORD God said, '*It is not good* for the man to be alone; I will make him a helper suitable for him'" (emphasis added).

When God said the man was "not good" without the woman, He was noting that the man was incomplete without his female counterpart. Man needs woman; woman needs man; the human family requires male and female; and God intends to do His work in the earth with both sexes.

Chauvinistic men might be tempted to think that God was giving men permission to dominate women when he called Eve a "helper." Think again! The Hebrew word used here for *helper*, *ezer*, is actually the same Hebrew word to describe God fourteen times in the Old Testament.[4] It does not imply inferiority. This passage underscores the principle of biblical equality.

We see this principle of God using both men and women side by side in many places throughout the Bible: Deborah and Barak, Ruth and Boaz, Esther and Mordecai are prime examples. We also see God elevating women to a place of value and significance even though they were put at a disadvantage by the curse of sin after Adam and Eve's fall from grace. After the fall in Eden, God said to the woman in Genesis 3:16, "I will greatly multiply your pain in childbirth, in pain you will bring forth children; yet your desire will be for your husband, and he will rule over you."

This passage does not imply that women are inferior, or that they have been relegated by God to a position of subservience. Rather, it shows us the reality of life under the bondage of sin. Wherever sin rules, women will suffer from the pain of domination, abuse and oppression. You can see this reality anywhere in the world today, particularly in countries where Christian influence is minimal. Women face a great deal of pain, but when Jesus came He not only paid for our sins but also overcame this curse. This is why I tell women all over the world that the promise of Christ's forgiveness in John 3:16 nullifies the pain of Genesis 3:16.

And because of redemption through Christ, women now have the equal opportunity to know God and to participate with Him in His mission to save the world. Sarah is a wonderful forerunner of this truth. When God called her and her husband to go to Canaan, she packed up her things and left all that was familiar. When God spoke to her husband about a promised heir, she chose to believe with him. She and Abraham held hands throughout this long, laborious journey. And in the end, when the writer of Hebrews gives out the awards to Old Testament characters for strongest faith, both Abraham and Sarah take center stage. After praising Abraham, Hebrews 11:11–12 says:

> By faith even Sarah herself received ability to conceive, even beyond the proper time of life, since she considered Him faithful who had promised. Therefore there was born even of one man, and him as good as dead at that, as many descendants as the stars of heaven in number, and innumerable as the sand which is by the seashore.

The miracle of Isaac's birth was not attributed to Abraham alone. Sarah got equal billing. And she was not just a biological receptacle for Abraham's seed. God did not call Sarah just because He needed a womb. He needed Sarah's faith, too. This passage in Hebrews says Sarah exercised her faith to conceive, and she considered God faithful. She had her own personal relationship with the Lord, and this ended up changing history forever. One man and one woman following God together made all the difference.

During Abraham and Sarah's arduous faith journey, we can see there was a war over Sarah's destiny. God had a plan to use Sarah as a mother of faith, but the enemy also targeted her and tried to put roadblocks in front of her. Right after the couple began their trek across the wilderness, they fled to Egypt to find provision during a famine. While there, Abram lied about Sarai's true identity—and she almost ended up in bed with Pharaoh! God intervened supernaturally by striking Pharaoh's house with plagues, and Sarai was spared.

This same scenario was repeated much later when Abraham lied to Abimelech about Sarah's identity. Abimelech would have tried to make Sarah his sexual partner, but this time God came to Abimelech in a dream and said: "You are a dead man because of the woman whom you have taken, for she is married" (Genesis 20:3). In both of these situations, God stepped in to protect the woman He had called to be a pioneer. He waged war for her, and defended her not only from evil men but also from her own husband's poor judgment.

This should make it clear that God does not put men on a higher plane than women, or place more value on them. God created males and females as equals, and both sexes have a significant part to play in His divine plan. The amazing plan of redemption, which began with Abraham and Sarah, required obedience and faith from both of them. God has called men and women as faith partners.

You may struggle to believe this because of your own life experience. You may have been pushed around by men all your life; you may have been ignored, neglected or viewed as inferior; you may have been sexually violated by men; you may have been rejected or abandoned by your father.

You may wonder: *If God intervened to protect Sarah from Pharaoh, why didn't He protect me from the relative who molested me, the boyfriend who raped me or the husband who beat me? Or you may ask: If women are important to God, why does it seem I have spent most of my time on the sidelines?*

It is okay to ask these things, but you must let your questions lead you to the arms of Christ. Like Sarah, you must be willing to look beyond the barrenness of your situation. You must exercise faith in an amazing God who transcends your negative life experiences. And you may be required to leave your comfortable surroundings—and the pain of your past—to follow Him.

I love the fact that the mother of our faith was barren. It was scientifically impossible for her to have a child, yet God's word to Sarah overrode the facts. She dared to believe. Her womb was dead, but she put her trust in the Life Giver. And by doing so she became a role model of biblical faith for all of us. I encourage you to follow her example and be a pioneer.

─────────── LET'S TALK ABOUT IT ───────────

1. Sarah had her own relationship with God. When did you begin your journey with God and become a born-again Christian? (If you have not had this experience, you can go to the appendix for more information about how to begin the Christian life. Ask a close friend or members of your group to pray with you.)
2. Sarah is the mother of our faith. Do you have any spiritual mothers in your life? Describe a woman who has modeled the Christian faith for you and what qualities you admire in her.
3. God has always used women in His redemptive plan. But sometimes well-meaning Christians imply that He prefers to use men, or that women are His secondary choice. Have you ever been tempted to believe this? Why?
4. Sarah had to leave the comforts of her life in Ur in order to obey God. She also had to believe God's promise even when everything in the natural said she was too old to have a baby. Are you asking God to do something that seems impossible? Share your dream with the group.

──── A MESSAGE FROM YOUR HEAVENLY FATHER ────

My precious daughter,
I have called you to follow Me. Be willing to leave all that is comfortable and familiar so you can align yourself

with My plan. I have a great adventure for you that is far more exciting than you have ever imagined. Just as I used Sarah to become a mother of nations, I want to use you to influence people for Me. Receive My promise and let it take root in your heart. Trust Me even when times are difficult. Don't get discouraged by looking at your circumstances, your age, your family problems, your failures, your flaws or your limitations. I am bigger than any of those things. Put your trust in Me and consider Me faithful, even as Sarah believed My promise even though she was barren. Let Me use you as a pioneer. Let Me birth My promises in you.

2

The Five Daughters of Zelophehad

The Courage to Challenge Tradition

There is no improving the future without disturb-
ing the present.

—Catherine Booth (1829–1890),
preacher and cofounder of The Salvation Army
with her husband, William

As a child growing up in segregated Alabama, Rosa Parks
came to understand the power of cultural tradition. When
she attended grade school in the 1920s, white kids rode a bus and
black children walked. That was the rule. Racism was a cruel way
of life. Once, her grandfather had to guard the front door of her
house with a shotgun because Ku Klux Klan members were march-
ing on her street. One of the schools she attended, which was
founded by Northern whites to help black youth, was burned twice
by arsonists.[1] This was one reason fewer than 7 percent of African

Americans had a high school diploma at the time Parks graduated from high school.

During her childhood she never imagined riding a bus anywhere. Describing the school buses of her youth, she said: "I'd see the bus pass every day. . . . But to me, that was a way of life; we had no choice but to accept what was the custom. The bus was among the first ways I realized there was a black world and a white world."[2]

When Parks began working for a department store in the city of Montgomery in the 1950s, she had to learn the rules of the racist game. The first four rows of seats on all city buses were reserved for white people—even though 75 percent of bus riders in the city were black. African Americans were allowed to sit in the middle sections of the buses until more whites boarded; if more seats were needed by whites, a sign notified blacks to sit farther to the back, or stand.

Rosa made history and triggered national protest on the evening of December 1, 1955, at around six o'clock, when she refused to vacate her seat on the Cleveland Avenue bus. The bus driver, James F. Blake, approached her and ordered her and three other blacks to move. The other three complied, but Rosa wrote in her memoirs that she sensed an unusual resolve at that moment: "When that white driver stepped back toward us, when he waved his hand and ordered us up and out of our seats, I felt a determination cover my body like a quilt on a winter night."[3]

When Parks refused, the driver told her: "Well, if you don't stand up, I'm going to have to call the police and have you arrested." She told Blake in a matter-of-fact tone: "You may do that."[4]

And thus began one of the most turbulent eras in American history—a time when antiquated Jim Crow laws were abolished and traditions of racial inequality were dismantled. The struggle was not easy. It was an era of bombings, police brutality, peaceful sit-ins, passionate speeches, horrifying assassinations and national repentance. It ended with the passage of a sweeping civil rights law. And one brave woman's willingness to challenge the status quo fueled the movement.

Some people later downplayed Parks's actions on that Montgomery bus, saying that she refused to move simply because she was tired. She responded to this accusation in her autobiography, *My Story*: "People always say that I didn't give up my seat because I was tired, but that isn't true. I was not tired physically, or no more tired than I usually was at the end of a working day. I was not old, although some people have an image of me as being old then. I was 42. No, the only tired I was, was tired of giving in."[5]

Whenever I read about Rosa Parks, or any of the other less-famous people (including many other women) who helped end legalized segregation, I think about five women in the Bible who deserve much more credit than they receive. They are known as the daughters of Zelophehad, and they are mentioned in the Scriptures in five different places (see Numbers 26:33; 27:1; 36:11; Joshua 17:3; and 1 Chronicles 7:15). These girls—Mahlah, Noah, Hoglah, Milcah and Tirzah—must have been special. I call them the first feminists in history.

Just as Rosa Parks grew up in an era of injustice, the daughters of Zelophehad grew up in an era when women were not treated fairly. They were young girls during the time when the Israelites were wandering in the wilderness of Sinai. Every day they heard people talking about what life would be like when they arrived in Canaan, the "land of milk and honey." But it did not sound much like a land of promise to Zelophehad's girls. Men spoke of obtaining portions of land on the other side of the Jordan River so they could plant crops, herd cattle, dig for precious metals and build fortunes. But the daughters of Zelophehad knew they would not inherit anything in their new home.

The problem was with the law. In patriarchal Israel, only men were allowed to own property. And because of this reality, a family with no male heir had no chance of obtaining inheritance rights once Canaan was conquered. If a man had only daughters, his family line essentially ended and his daughters were given no portion in the new land. This was the rule of the day. Women were told plainly: "You don't get any."

Yet when we meet the daughters of Zelophehad, we learn that they did not sit back and accept this cultural edict. Like Rosa Parks, these women did not go with the flow. Numbers 27:2–4 tells us:

> They stood before Moses and before Eleazar the priest and before the leaders and all the congregation, at the doorway of the tent of meeting, saying, "Our father died in the wilderness, yet he was not among the company of those who gathered themselves together against the LORD in the company of Korah; but he died in his own sin, and he had no sons. Why should the name of our father be withdrawn from among his family because he had no son? Give us a possession among our father's brothers."

The Bible does not give us the background of this story. We do not know the conversations that went on behind closed doors in Zelophehad's home. We do not know how these girls shaped their strong opinions. We do not know why they grew up to be so brave in a culture where women had no rights. We do not know how long they rehearsed their speech or which girl made it. We do know that most women of that time period spent most of their days fetching water, washing clothes, tending to animals and cooking. Women were devalued and marginalized. With the exception of Miriam,

Moses' sister, we have no record of any other women in prominent leadership during that time period.

Yet these girls emerge as true examples of bravery. They were willing to ask a question that had never been asked. They challenged the system. They were so fearless, in fact, that they went all the way to Moses to make their audacious request. I am sure they were intimidated by the appeal process, and by the attitudes of people who felt their crusade was improper, but this did not stop them.

The Bible does not paint Zelophehad's daughters as rebels. They did not come to Moses with a vindictive spirit or an angry tone. They were not burning bras, carrying protest signs or screaming obscenities. We have every reason to believe their campaign was a righteous one, and that their words were delivered with grace as well as courage. Not only did Moses listen to them and treat them with respect, but God heard their request and acted on their behalf. Numbers 27:5–7 says:

> So Moses brought their case before the LORD. Then the LORD spoke to Moses, saying, "The daughters of Zelophehad are right in their statements. You shall surely give them a hereditary possession among their father's brothers, and you shall transfer the inheritance of their father to them."

I hope you understand the weight of these words. Almighty God said: "The daughters of Zelophehad are right." In this complicated dispute, with the majority firmly against the concept of sexual equality, the Lord lowered the gavel of heaven and ruled in favor of women! He contradicted centuries of patriarchal tradition. God Almighty opposed a cultural precedent. And as a result of this divine edict (and Moses' willingness to obey it), the laws of Israel were changed in order to reflect the values of God's Kingdom.

Whatever Happened to Spunk?

If the daughters of Zelophehad only appeared in the Bible once, we might be tempted to overlook them, or to dismiss their actions as abnormal. But, as I have noted, they are mentioned in Scripture in five places, and always in a positive light. It is obvious God wants to say something to us through the lives of these primitive reformers.

Many modern Christians, in an honorable effort to promote conservative family values, have erroneously taught that women can best please Christ if they are passive, demure and always focused on domestic duties. The subtle message is: Women should stay in the background, support their husbands, raise nice kids and keep their mouths shut so that men can be the heroes.

This is a laughable philosophy when you compare it to the biblical record. The Bible is full of gutsy women who stuck their necks out to speak when it was not culturally proper. Heaven smiled on these women. And God knows we need more of them today. Yet many women have told me horror stories of how they were treated by other Christians when they decided to take a bold initiative.

We need more women with spunk, which is defined in the dictionary as "courage in the face of difficulty; spirit." Courage is not a masculine quality; it transcends gender. But in many churches today, women do not feel they have permission to be courageous. They are told, "This is a man's job in a man's world."

As a man I can admire the courage of a martyr like William Tyndale (who was burned at the stake for translating the Bible into English) or a missionary like William Carey (who pioneered the work of the Gospel in India). But it does not make me any less of a man if I admire the bravery of a woman like Corrie ten Boom, who suffered for her Christian faith in a German prison camp because she illegally hid Jews in her home in Holland during World

War II. Corrie's courage had nothing to do with her gender, but it certainly made her more like Jesus.

Proverbs 28:1 says: "The wicked flee when no one is pursuing, but the righteous are bold as a lion." Notice this verse attaches no gender to the character quality. It is not only righteous men who are urged to be bold; righteous women are also called to be fearless. So the question remains: Why do Christian women struggle with the idea of being spunky? Some may have been accused of being tomboys when they were younger if they showed any leadership ability. Some may have been made to feel they were misguided to have big dreams or aspire to leadership positions.

When my own daughters were young, they loved to watch the Disney cartoon *Mulan*, the story of a Chinese girl who lived during the time of the ancient Han dynasty. It is a cute story complete with a rap-singing dragon, a spectacular avalanche and lots of fireworks, but its serious message of sexual equality made a big impression on my girls when they were preteens.

When the emperor requires all men in China, including Mulan's elderly father, to enlist in the army to fight the invading Huns, she disguises herself as a young man named Ping and runs off to battle in her father's place. She struggles to fit into the world of male soldiers, and eventually her deception is uncovered. Yet in the end she saves the day by exposing the Huns' plot to assassinate the emperor. He honors her in front of the nation, and in the end she gets to marry the handsome warrior, Li Shang, who had chastised her for coming to the battlefield.

Mulan is fanciful and farfetched, and the Disneyfied romance at the end of the tale seems to tell girls subconsciously that their real goal is always to marry the prince. But this cartoon warrior has more depth than previous Disney princesses such as the poor Cinderella or the airheaded Ariel in *The Little Mermaid*. Mulan has more backbone than all of those delicate girls put together—not because she disguises herself as a man but because she does something outrageously daring to protect her family. Mulan shows millions of girls that it is okay to have spunk.

In many Christian churches, women have sometimes been taught (by other women, mostly) that God wants them to be passive. They often refer to 1 Peter 3:1–4, which says:

> In the same way, you wives, be submissive to your own husbands so that even if any of them are disobedient to the word, they may be won without a word by the behavior of their wives, as they observe your chaste and respectful behavior. Your adornment must not be *merely* external—braiding the hair, and wearing gold jewelry, or putting on dresses; but let it be the hidden person of the heart, *with the imperishable quality of a gentle and quiet spirit*, which is precious in the sight of God.
>
> emphasis added

Bible scholars believe that Peter is contrasting godly Christian women with the prostitutes of the day, who often wore elaborate hairstyles that included interwoven pearls and gold jewelry. Peter is saying, in essence, "Don't focus on the externals of your appearance—it's what's inside that counts!" The passage is primarily an exhortation to women to develop the character of Christ, the epitome of meekness, gentleness and purity. Peter urges the women of the first century not to be rebellious, quarrelsome, brash or sexually provocative.

Sadly, this passage is misused to suggest that *silence* or *passivity* is a virtue. But that is never the message of Scripture. God often calls people to speak and act for Him, and He commands us never to live in fear. Many times He calls women to speak for Him, and they have a responsibility to overcome their fears and obey His mandate. A woman who is mousy or timid does not reflect the character of Jesus.

This is underscored in the remainder of the passage in 1 Peter 3:5–6:

> For in this way in former times the holy women also, who hoped in God, used to adorn themselves, being submissive to their own husbands; just as Sarah obeyed Abraham, calling him lord, and you have become her children if you do what is right *without being frightened by any fear.*
>
> emphasis added

Notice the last sentence: If women want to please God and be considered "children of Sarah," they must renounce fear! Fear is not allowed in a godly woman's life. When women gather for Bible studies or conferences, they often focus on topics like submission, domesticity, modesty or family issues. But when Peter ends his comments to women, he makes it clear that they are also called to be fearless. This is a major part of the Holy Spirit's agenda for women.

Blaze a Trail for Others

Rosa Parks was awarded the Congressional Gold Medal and the President's Medal of Freedom for her civil rights work. When she died in 2005, she was the first woman and the second African American to lie in state in the United States Capitol rotunda, and fifty thousand mourners walked past her coffin to pay their respects. At one of her memorial services, then-United States Secretary of State Condoleezza Rice—another African American woman from Alabama—told the crowd that if Rosa had not broken the barriers of race in 1955, she herself probably would not have become the most high-profile woman in the United States government.[6]

Rosa Parks not only triggered the Montgomery Bus Boycott and the ensuing Civil Rights movement, but she inspired a generation of younger women to carry the torch of freedom further than she could. Condoleezza Rice, the daughter of a Presbyterian minister, was only one year old when Parks refused to give up her seat on a bus. But acknowledging that woman's courage, Rice earned a Ph.D. from the University of Denver and became the first female and the first person from a minority race to become a provost at Stanford University. She also became a celebrated expert on Soviet affairs—she learned the Russian language—years before she was called upon to serve in the administration of former president George W. Bush.[7]

The lesson here: You never know whom you may inspire to follow after you. Actions have consequences. Rosa Parks blazed a trail for many other women who wanted a place on a bus. One woman's courage inspired a schoolgirl named Condoleezza; that schoolgirl faced her own fears and broke down more walls for other generations.

This is certainly what happened with the daughters of Zelophehad. Their story does not end with their meeting with Moses. They appear again in the book of Joshua, after the death of Moses, after the Israelites have entered Canaan. Moses had promised them an inheritance in the Land of Promise, but they had to wander in the wilderness until a faithless generation had died. Then, the Bible says, they came to Joshua to remind him of their legal right. Joshua 17:4–6 says:

> They came near before Eleazar the priest and before Joshua the son of Nun and before the leaders, saying, "The LORD commanded Moses to give us an inheritance among our brothers." So according to the command of the LORD he gave them an inheritance among their father's brothers. Thus there fell ten portions to Manasseh,

besides the land of Gilead and Bashan, which is beyond the Jordan, because the daughters of Manasseh received an inheritance among his sons. And the land of Gilead belonged to the rest of the sons of Manasseh.

The daughters of Zelophehad came to Joshua at the time he was dividing Canaan among Israel's twelve tribes. It is important to notice the mathematical details of this passage in Joshua 17. Zelophehad was part of a tribe that had six clans, but his family tree was barren, in a sense, because he had no male heirs. If Joshua had applied standard inheritance law to the situation, Zelophehad's family would have received no territory, and the tribe of Manasseh would have been awarded only five portions.

But that is not what happened. God intervened through the courage of these five women. They dared to ask for a new ruling, and God answered by contradicting culture. The law was reformed. In the end, the tribe of Manasseh was awarded not five but ten portions—making them one of the largest landowners in Israel. The size of the territory was doubled. And all this was because some spunky girls dared to ask a question that had never been asked in Israel.

God is definitely in the details of this story. If you examine it closely, you find that five portions of Manasseh are represented by Abiezer, Helek, Asriel, Shechem, Hepher and Shemida while the five additional ones are represented by Mahlah, Noah, Hoglah, Milcah and Tirzah. That's five men and five women! It creates a beautiful picture of sexual equality and partnership.

I have often challenged church leaders to realize that if they would be willing to discard antiquated ideas of male dominance (as Moses did) and be open to giving women a spiritual inheritance (as Joshua did), then they could double their impact. If we challenge women to become fearless—and to get involved in all areas of ministry—we will win twice as many people to Christ, cast out twice as many devils, see twice as many miracles, send out twice as many missionaries and influence twice as many nations with the Gospel.

Let's Talk about It

1. Rosa Parks faced many obstacles, yet at the right time she challenged them. Is there a social issue that regularly concerns you? How could you use your faith to address this issue?
2. Women are sometimes discouraged from taking initiative or showing courage. This can even happen in churches. Did this ever happen to you? Share your experience.
3. Many women struggle with fear—of speaking in public, of making relationships or of trying new things. Can you identify a fear you know God wants you to overcome?
4. Have you ever done anything that you considered brave or daring? Share what happened. How did the people around you react to your behavior?

A Message from Your Heavenly Father

My precious daughter,

I have placed a beautiful land of promise in front of you. As a loving Father, I have left an inheritance for you. I would never deny you that inheritance because you are a woman. It is My good pleasure to give you the Kingdom. I invite you to be bold enough to ask for all I have for you. Come boldly before My throne and don't be passive. Some people would like to keep you from receiving My inheritance. They may even have used intimidation, manipulation or fear to shut you down. You are not accountable to those people. You are accountable to Me. I am calling you forward. I want you to be bold. I want you to step out of your weakness and into My courage. You can't do this in your own strength, but I will empower you as you trust Me. Let go of your fears. Put on My armor, feast on My words and allow Me to strengthen you with My Spirit. I will make you a fearless woman.

3

Ruth, the Moabite

The Courage to Forsake the Past

> I'm going to scream from the mountaintop until
> the day I die that God will redeem any life, save
> any soul and use anybody who will cooperate
> with Him. I know because I know what He did
> for me—and He didn't have anything good to
> work with here.
>
> —Bible teacher Beth Moore

If you are like me, you do not enjoy reading genealogies in the
Bible. Endless lists of names tend to put me to sleep. But I have
learned that those names are there for a reason, and if we tune our
ears to hear from the Holy Spirit, we can learn important things
from seemingly insignificant details. This is especially true of the
genealogy that appears at the beginning of Matthew's gospel. In

tracing the lineage of Joseph, the husband of the virgin Mary, we are told:

> Judah was the father of Perez and Zerah by Tamar, Perez was the father of Hezron, and Hezron the father of Ram. Ram was the father of Amminadab, Amminadab the father of Nahshon, and Nahshon the father of Salmon. Salmon was the father of Boaz by Rahab, Boaz was the father of Obed by Ruth, and Obed the father of Jesse. Jesse was the father of David the king. David was the father of Solomon by Bathsheba who had been the wife of Uriah.
>
> Matthew 1:3–6

God reveals His amazing mercy in the details of this list. Notice that among these descendants of Abraham, four women are mentioned. This is highly unusual since women were rarely listed in genealogies during the time of Christ. What is even more striking is the type of women who are included. For one thing, three of the four women are Gentiles—and although Bathsheba was probably a Jew, her husband was a Hittite. So much for "racial purity" in Christ's lineage.

Secondly, each of the women mentioned represents a moral scandal. Tamar's relationship with Judah, her father-in-law, was illicit (she posed as a prostitute and he slept with her, and then tried to cover up his sin before he was exposed); Rahab ran a brothel in Jericho; David had an adulterous affair with Bathsheba (and then had her husband killed to cover his tracks). And Ruth? She was from Moab—a land outside the borders of Israel that was founded by Lot through an incestuous relationship with his older daughter.

Prostitution. Incest. Adultery. This sounds more like *The Jerry Springer Show* or *Desperate Housewives* than a biblical narrative! But it reveals another amazing thing about the Bible: Scripture does not offer us a sanitized view of life. The Bible is raw. It tells us how God works with broken, sinful people, and it does not mask their problems or hide their flaws. It should comfort all of us that Jesus Christ's earthly family had plenty of skeletons in its primitive closets. He was born into a dysfunctional family—and that should give hope to all of us who need forgiveness and cleansing from the ugly secrets of our past.

Ruth stands alone as the most unlikely person in the Old Testament to stumble into the grace of God. She was an outcast (Israelites hated the Moabites because of their dubious origins), and when we first meet her she is a pitiful widow with no children. In Old Testament times, this meant she was financially destitute and socially stigmatized. Women in those days were valued only if they had a male attached to them—either a husband or a son. Ruth had neither.

To make matters worse, the only real friend she had in the world—her Jewish mother-in-law, Naomi—was in even more pitiful condition. Naomi's husband had also died, along with her two sons, so she, too, was hopeless. She was so discouraged by her predicament that she told Ruth and her other daughter-in-law, Orpah, that she should change her name from *Naomi* (which means "pleasant") to *Mara* (which means "bitter").

But even though Naomi was at her lowest point, Ruth somehow saw a glimmer of hope in her mother-in-law—who had a relationship with the true God. (Remember: People are watching you when you are going through tough times, and even if you feel discouraged they can see how you trust Him.) When Naomi decided to return to the land of Israel to seek a new life, Ruth made one of the boldest decisions recorded in the Bible. Even though she was a Moabite, she decided to forsake the land of her birth and the religious practices of her family so she could follow her mother-in-law to a strange land where the people worshiped Jehovah.

Ruth made a courageous declaration of faith to Naomi:

> But Ruth said, "Do not urge me to leave you or turn back from following you; for where you go, I will go, and where you lodge, I will lodge. Your people shall be my people, and your God, my God."
>
> Ruth 1:16

This was not a flippant decision to hitch a ride with Naomi and find a new job across the border. This was her moment of conversion. A Gentile from the land of Moab decided to forsake everything she knew in order to serve her mother-in-law's God. She made a 180-degree turn that would alter her destiny forever—and make biblical history. She was forsaking everything Moabite and adopting a Hebrew way of life. She was leaving the idols of her family and choosing to worship the God of Abraham, Isaac and Jacob.

Her poignant story (one of only two books of the Bible named for a woman) is considered one of the most brilliant examples of Hebrew literature. In four short chapters, this social outcast from Moab is eventually accepted by people in Bethlehem. She finds herself in the fields of Boaz, a distant relative of Naomi, and he sympathizes with her. Before the end of the tale, Naomi convinces Ruth to propose to Boaz (this was unheard of in those times), Boaz decides to marry her, and in the end Ruth gives birth to a Jewish child who ends up being the grandfather of King David. The girl who was literally the last in line to receive favor from God was moved to the front.

The book of Ruth, in theological terms, carries an obvious message—showing that God's mercy and love were never meant to be reserved for Jews only. God always had it in His plan to extend forgiveness to Gentiles, and Ruth is a prime example. But Ruth also carries a special message for women, especially those with a past they are not proud of. She, like no other Bible character, reveals just how far God will go to redeem us.

You Must Leave Moab

To fully understand the miracle of God's mercy extended to Ruth, we must go back in Israel's history and study the tension that existed between God's people and the Moabites. This Gentile nation, which was situated on the eastern shores of the Dead Sea in modern Jordan, began when Lot's oldest daughter got him drunk and had intercourse with him in order to produce an heir. This is not exactly the kind of story you want to include in the family scrapbook! The shame associated with that dirty deed laid a shaky foundation for Moab's future.

Later in the Old Testament narrative we learn that the Moabites cursed Israel as they were attempting to enter Canaan. They were worshipers of the pagan god Chemosh, whose religion involved human sacrifice, sexual immorality and witchcraft. In fact, the sorcerer Balaam was recruited by Moab's king, Balak, to curse God's people and lure them astray. For this reason, God told Moses that the Moabites were to be completely cut off from the righteous Israelites:

> No Ammonite or Moabite shall enter the assembly of the LORD; none of their descendants, even to the tenth generation, shall ever enter the assembly of the LORD, because they did not meet you with food and water on the way when you came out of Egypt, and because they hired against you Balaam the son of Beor from Pethor of Mesopotamia, to curse you.
>
> Deuteronomy 23:3–4

This is the ugly backdrop for Ruth's story. She lives among a people who are not even allowed to enter God's presence because of their sinful history. Her parents were probably worshipers of Chemosh and other idols. They most likely practiced witchcraft. She may have grown up hearing about the reputation of Lot's daughters (who are not even named in the biblical narrative). Incest and other forms of sexual sin were prevalent in Moab.

Yet Ruth chose to swim against the current. Even though her sister, Orpah, remained in Moab, Ruth left her comfort zone and rejected what was familiar. She was probably not aware that Moses had forbidden Moabites to worship the true God; yet even if she had heard this news, she decided to take a chance anyway. She wanted out. And she knew that when she left Moab for Bethlehem, she was never coming back to her surroundings. She was leaving everything behind.

We would all do well to emulate Ruth's fierce determination. Many people choose to follow Christ, but not everyone is willing to take up his or her cross and forsake all. Many Christians embrace the Gospel intellectually, and they begin attending church or doing religious exercises, but they are still carrying the shame of their pasts. They try to worship God while still living in Moab, or they drag the baggage of Moab with them to Bethlehem.

I often meet Christian women who are tormented by memories—either of their own sins or of sinful things done to them. One of these women, Sheryl, came to me for prayer at a conference in Illinois. Her painful story was familiar. When she was eight years old, her four brothers began sexually abusing her when her parents were not home. They took turns with her for fun. To them, it was just experimentation, and their sister was the equipment they used. They had no idea how their behavior was scarring her emotionally.

The nightmarish abuse with her brothers ended when Sheryl was in the fourth grade, but only after she stood at the top of the stairs in her home and shouted to her mother: "Please don't leave me with him!" She was speaking of her oldest brother, who was the ringleader in the abuse and who sometimes brought a neighbor boy to the house to join in the sex games.

The abuse made Sheryl sexually curious, confused and horribly devalued. She tells in her own words what happened next:

> Throughout my childhood I was a toy to the neighborhood boys. I felt like everyone knew. None of the neighborhood girls wanted to play with me. My parents divorced when I was twelve. My brother brought home a friend from the army named Al. He was nineteen, and he flirted with my mom and she accepted it. While he was in a relationship with my mom, he told me he was going to teach me how to treat a man sexually. On our living room couch in December 1983 I gave, and he took. My sexual relationship with Al continued until I was fifteen, when my mom left him. Of course, this did nothing for our mother/daughter relationship.[1]

Thankfully, Sheryl found Jesus in 1989. While attending Bible college, she heard a visiting preacher talk about the importance of being healed from the past. This was the first time Sheryl faced "it"—she had never told anyone about her abuse. "This was the first time in my life I had admitted it," Sheryl says. "My friend Jennifer held me as I cried and screamed in agony. I could see demons reaching out to grab me, but they couldn't touch me." That experience, coupled with some counseling she received two years later, got Sheryl on what she calls "the long road to recovery" from sexual abuse. She eventually confronted each of her brothers and forgave them for what they had done to her. And today she carries a special burden to see abused women healed from trauma.

I have met many "Sheryls" who have been emotionally and spiritually crippled by various forms of abuse, or by the shame they carry for mistakes they have made. Each situation is uniquely heartbreaking, but the patterns are similar. In my years of ministering in women's conferences around the world I have determined that the devil really only has a few tricks in his bag, and he uses these over and over to destroy women. As you read over this list, you may identify some baggage from your past that you are still carrying:

1. *Sexual abuse.* For some women, like Sheryl, this happens when they are children—and another family member is often the perpetrator. Abuse of this nature is never addressed; it is always swept under the rug. Women are expected to keep quiet about it, and in some cases they are threatened with punishment if they ever reveal what happened.

   Women who suffer the traumatic effects of sexual abuse (it is estimated that 30 percent of women in the United States have been abused) often blame themselves for what happened.[2] A deceptive voice whispers: "That man did that to you because you invited him to, or because you deserved this." This causes the shame to increase, and can lead to depression, mental problems and self-destructive behavior.

   Thankfully, a woman who runs into the arms of Jesus can find not only spiritual salvation but also emotional healing from the wounds of abuse. The Holy Spirit can help her stop believing the lies that keep her in a prison of shame.

2. *Physical or verbal abuse.* Domestic abuse is the single greatest cause of injury to women in this country. Some studies show that a woman in the United States is beaten every 7.4 seconds.[3] If you have endured this kind of cruelty, or are involved in an abusive relationship now, your emotions are raw and your soul is scarred. Abused women also tend to blame themselves for what happened to them. Abuse causes the victim to lose any sense of self-worth.

The good news is that Jesus reached out to abused women during His earthly ministry, and He is still offering His healing today. It will require a woman to leave an abusive relationship (even if she is married), but through counseling and prayer she can find complete restoration.

3. *Fornication or adultery.* If you allowed yourself to be pulled into a sexual relationship outside of marriage—or if you were the aggressor in such a relationship—you will struggle with feelings of guilt. But regardless of how many sexual partners you have had, God can give you the grace to live a pure life now. Even if you feel like trash, or if other people called you trash, Jesus can recycle the mess you made of your life and make it into something beautiful.

4. *Abortion.* Even though our society has made abortion legal, and people view it as an acceptable way to end an unwanted pregnancy, women who abort their babies struggle with unwanted shame. Many suffer from emotional as well as physical trauma after the procedure. If you are in this category, God wants you to come clean. Through full confession, repentance and healing prayer, you can be free from the heaviness you feel.

5. *Lesbianism.* Many environmental as well as generational factors can pull a person into a gay lifestyle. Many women are drawn into lesbianism because men abused them, and, therefore, they associate men with pain and violence. For these women, it is safer to seek intimacy from a woman because she is gentle and tender. That is understandable, but it does not make it a healthy choice.

If you have lived in a homosexual lifestyle, or feel some level of same-sex attraction, this does not mean God hates you, or that you have to live this way. God is in the business of healing our emotional wounds, and He is well able to heal us sexually. You can find trusted Christian friends who will love you through the healing process, no matter how long it takes.

6. *Occult practices.* If you ever dabbled in occultism, or if you were ever involved in a false religion or New Age sect, you opened the door to unhealthy spiritual influences. Demons are real, and they seek to manipulate people through such things as ritual sacrifice, horoscopes, fortune-telling, Tarot cards, séances, crystals, chanting to idols, mantras and occult books. Any form of worship that is directed toward anything other than the true God, revealed in Jesus Christ, can result in spiritual bondage.

If you are involved in any such activities, or if you have paraphernalia from past involvement, you must make a clean break. You must have the courage to throw away items that could maintain your connection to the past. The Lord can help you be free.

7. *Depression or anxiety.* Women who suffer from low self-esteem battle depression regularly—and our culture says the best way to handle this is through drugs. There are certain types of clinical depression that may require medication for recovery, but in many cases taking a drug is only putting a Band-Aid on the problem.

Furthermore, women who wrestle with depression or anxiety disorders are often tempted to medicate their pain with excessive alcohol, prescription medicines or by cutting themselves. And they do these things in secret because it is too shameful to face the ugly truth they are hiding from. If you struggle with compulsive behaviors, you do not have to fight this battle alone. If you share your struggle with caring

Christian friends, they can help you discover the root causes of your brokenness and lead you into healing.

8. *Unforgiveness.* Many women who suffer from physical maladies such as cancer or chronic pain are actually sick because they have internalized their anger toward another person. Bitterness can make you ill. When you hate a person, or fantasize about bad things happening to them, you are not hurting them—you are only hurting yourself. Bitterness is like a poison that eventually eats us alive.

This is why Jesus gave us such a sobering ultimatum on forgiveness. He said He would turn us over to "the torturers" if we did not forgive from the heart (see Matthew 18:34–35). We will experience emotional torment if we hold resentment. As we forgive others, we are free to experience the forgiveness of God toward us.

No matter what injustices you have suffered, no matter how your father or uncle or grandfather treated you, no matter how your friends neglected you, no matter how wronged you were by a teacher or a boyfriend, you must abandon your toxic emotions and ask Jesus for the grace to forgive fully.

Follow Ruth's Steps

If anyone would have been considered ineligible to receive God's grace and forgiveness it would have been Ruth, yet she is a shining example of a woman who would not take no for an answer. In the first chapter of Ruth, she packed up her belongings and headed to Israel with Naomi, pledging to worship her God. In the second chapter, she discovered the kindness of God in the wheat fields of Boaz when he told his workmen to leave extra grain for her. In the third chapter, she became so bold that she went to Boaz's threshing floor at night and lay at his feet to ask him to marry her. (Because Naomi was Boaz's relative, Ruth was actually petitioning him to enact a law called the "kinsman obligation," in which the nearest relative to a widow marries her to protect the lineage.)

And in the last chapter of her story, this underprivileged girl from Moab married Boaz—and we hear a chorus of Israelites saying of her: "May the LORD make the woman who is coming into your home like Rachel and Leah, both of whom built the house of Israel; and may you achieve wealth in Ephrathah and become famous in Bethlehem" (Ruth 4:11). How did Ruth go from being a stigmatized pagan to a celebrated "daughter of Rachel and Leah"? She took the same path that you must take.

First, she left Moab. Because she wanted to serve the God of Israel, she was willing to forsake the past. She left the shame, the false gods, the deception and the lies of the land of her fathers. She was willing to leave her sister, Orpah, who lacked her determination. If you want to serve Christ fully, you must make a clean break from your past life. You cannot maintain a connection with it.

I have often thought of the journey Ruth and Naomi made from Moab to Bethlehem, realizing that they had to cross the Jordan River to reach their new home. This is significant. Not only is the Jordan River the point at which Joshua and the Hebrew pilgrims entered the Promised Land, it is also the place where Jesus was baptized in water by John. The Jordan represents the waters of baptism.

Many Christians struggle in their spiritual journeys because they did not stop at the Jordan. They did not realize how important water baptism is. It is not a ritual. Baptism is a spiritual exercise whereby we say good-bye to our old life and embrace the new. It is where we publicly renounce our past loyalties to selfishness, greed, lust, partying, anger, addictions and whatever else we were enslaved by when we were in the world. Baptism in water is essential for any Christian who wants to serve the Lord wholeheartedly.

Second, Ruth found a mentor in Naomi. This is so important for you as a growing Christian. God never intended for you to live the Christian life alone. He desires for you to live in community, and He wants to place spiritual mothers in your life who can help you in your journey. If you do not have a mentor, pray and ask the Lord to place one in your life. Ruth would never have made it to Bethlehem, nor would she have ever wandered into Boaz's fields, if Naomi had not been her close adviser. You cannot get where you need to be spiritually without mentors.

Third, Ruth discovered the Lord's compassion when she was in the fields of Boaz. She really had no idea how good the God of Israel was until Boaz and his kinsmen demonstrated generosity to her. She had heard of the goodness of the Lord from her mother-in-law, but she experienced it in Bethlehem. You must get to know the Lord by spending time with Him. You must become convinced that He is for you and not against you. You must build your confidence in the goodness of Jesus.

Fourth, Ruth was willing to go to the threshing floor where Boaz was sleeping. Ruth was defying tradition when she did this. She was also risking her life, because women did not just wander down to the threshing floors at night where men would be drinking and carousing. She put her trust in God, and she also trusted that Boaz was a moral man who would protect her. She mustered incredible courage to make her petition.

In the Bible, threshing floors are symbolic of the refining work of the Holy Spirit. John the Baptist said this of Jesus:

"As for me, I baptize you with water for repentance, but He who is coming after me is mightier than I, and I am not fit to remove His sandals; He will baptize you with the Holy Spirit and fire. His winnowing fork is in His hand, and *He will thoroughly clear His threshing floor*; and He will gather His wheat into the barn, but He will burn up the chaff with unquenchable fire."

Matthew 3:11–12, emphasis added

This passage shows us that the work of the Holy Spirit is not just about empowerment. He also comes to refine us. He comes with His winnowing fork, and He threshes us like grain to remove the chaff—the bad attitudes, bad behavior, selfishness, pride and corruption that defile us. When we come to the threshing floor and submit fully to the operation of the Spirit, we give Him permission to invade our privacy, open our closets, rummage through our drawers, pull back the carpets and expose our sins so that we can be more like Christ.

When Ruth came to the threshing floor seeking Boaz's hand in marriage, she also submitted herself to this holy refining process. She bowed in full submission, yet at the same time she staked her claim to ask for the impossible. As a result of her faith, she was grafted into the family of God and made a daughter of Israel. This, too, can be your portion as you forsake all to follow Christ.

——————— LET'S TALK ABOUT IT ———————

1. Four women are mentioned in the genealogy of Joseph, the husband of Mary, in Matthew 1. What is so unique about these four women, and why do you think God included them in this list?

2. Ruth was a Moabite, yet she chose to leave her people to follow Naomi to Israel. Why did this require courage on Ruth's part?

3. We must leave the baggage of the past behind when we decide to follow Christ. Share from your heart what you left when you became a Christian.

4. Review the list of "baggage" starting on page 60. Have you been crippled by abuse, or do you struggle with mistakes you have made? Ask your group to pray with you for freedom.

——— A MESSAGE FROM YOUR HEAVENLY FATHER ———

My precious daughter,

No matter what sins you have committed, and no matter how you were used or abused, I have covered you with the blood of My precious Son. Your past does not define you. I have redeemed you. My Son paid the full price for your sin and shame, and when you repent and ask Him into your life, I remove your sins as far as the east is from the west. My love covers a multitude of sins. When I look at you now, I do not see the blemishes of the past, or the mistakes, nor do I maintain a record of your past wrongs. You are a new creation in Christ. All things are made new. Because you chose to follow Me, I have given you a new nature. My Son lives in your heart, and I have covered you with a robe of righteousness. You can approach Me with confidence, and I will always receive you with open arms. You are My beloved daughter and I long to spend time with you.

❧ 4 ❧

Achsah, Daughter of Caleb

The Courage to Claim God's Blessing

> Let us more and more insist on raising funds of
> love, of kindness, of understanding, of peace.
> Money will come if we seek first the Kingdom
> of God. The rest will be given.
>
> —Mother Teresa (1910–1997),
> founder of the Missionaries of
> Charity in Calcutta, India

It must have been a special privilege to grow up in the house of Caleb, who was one of the most faithful of God's followers in the Old Testament. When Moses sent his twelve spies into Canaan, the majority of them came back whining and complaining about the size of the giants who lived there. They told Moses they felt like grasshoppers when they looked at the walled cities built by their hostile enemies.

But not Caleb. The walls of Jericho did not frighten him. He, along with Joshua, saw the Land of Promise through a different lens. Caleb had eyes of faith. Instead of dangers and roadblocks he saw potential, resources and opportunity. The Lord was angered by the weak faith of the ten spies who grumbled, but of Caleb He said:

> "My servant Caleb, because he has had a different spirit and has followed me fully, I will bring into the land which he entered, and his descendants shall take possession of it."
>
> Numbers 14:24

Caleb's faith did not wane as he grew older, even during the many battles that ensued. Forty-five years after his spying mission, when it was time for Joshua to apportion the land to the twelve tribes, Caleb made a speech in which he recounted the goodness of God throughout his adult life. His testimony is recorded in Joshua 14:7, 10–11:

> "I was forty years old when Moses the servant of the LORD sent me from Kadesh-barnea to spy out the land. . . . Now behold, the LORD has let me live, just as He spoke, these forty-five years. . . . I am eighty-five years old today. I am still as strong today as I was in the day Moses sent me; as my strength was then, so my strength is now, for war and for going out and coming in."

At age 85, this stalwart champion vowed to continue his battle. He assumed possession of the territory known as Hebron (the land that he originally visited with the spies 45 years earlier), and he announced decisive plans to conquer it. Even in his old age, doubt did not weaken his vigor. Retirement was not in his vocabulary. Nothing could stop him. He had a special relationship with Almighty God, and he knew that God wanted to give this land to His people.

We should not be surprised to discover that Caleb's daughter, Achsah, learned a few things about faith from her father. Can you imagine what it would have been like for this young girl to sit at the dinner table each day and listen to Caleb's conversations? This man did not fear giants—and he imparted his courage to his children. This girl (whose name literally means "ankle bracelet") would grow up to become an enterprising woman of faith. Her story has an important lesson for all women.

After Caleb received his inheritance in Canaan, he issued a challenge to the men of the region. He offered to give his daughter's hand in marriage to the first man who would attack and capture the enemy stronghold of Kiriath-sepher (see Joshua 15:16). This may seem like an odd way to engineer a wedding proposal, but, in Old Testament times, it was Caleb's strategy to ensure that his beloved daughter did not end up with just any status quo husband—or a faithless coward. Caleb wanted the best for his girl, so he raised the bar. He wanted her to marry a champion.

When the young man named Othniel accepted Caleb's challenge and bravely overtook the pagan town, the focus of the story shifts to Achsah. Joshua 15:17–19 says:

> Othniel the son of Kenaz, the brother of Caleb, captured it; so he gave him Achsah his daughter as a wife. It came about that when she came to him, she persuaded him to ask her father for a field. So she alighted from the donkey, and Caleb said to her, "What do you want?" Then she said, "Give me a blessing; since you have given me the land of the Negev, give me also springs of water." So he gave her the upper springs and the lower springs.

There is a great deal of family drama buried between the lines of this obscure Bible story. Achsah was not a pushover. She was probably as strong-willed and determined as her daddy. She thought

71

like him. And deep inside, she had the same desire to inherit the Land of Promise and establish God's righteous rule in the midst of Canaan. Meanwhile, Caleb adored his little girl and wanted only the best for her.

So when she married Othniel, she first asked her husband to request land. That is understandable, since many marriages in Old Testament times included a deed transfer. But notice that Achsah was not satisfied with the normal transaction. After her father agreed to give the acreage she requested, she went out of her way to make a special request—and she made this entreaty herself. She knew the arid desert land of the Negev needed water to become fruitful, so she asked her father for access to a spring.

What happened next was almost comical. This brave, strong-willed patriarch melted like butter in the hands of his determined daughter. He not only gave her a spring, but the upper and the lower springs! He gave her a double portion of water, thereby assuring her success. He went beyond the norm and blessed her with abundance.

This story is especially interesting when you consider that Caleb had three sons (Iru, Elah and Naam are mentioned in 1 Chronicles 4:15), but in the narrative in Joshua the focus is on his only daughter—and we are never told what inheritance the boys received. I am sure their portion was substantial. But I find it striking that the Scripture singles out Caleb's generosity toward his daughter—whose faith and zeal are rewarded so lavishly. It should encourage any woman who wonders if God considers her a second-string player in His Kingdom. God loves His girls!

The story of Achsah reminds me of some of the interactions I had with my daughters when they were growing up. When my girls were in school we lived in a suburban neighborhood and I had a middle-class salary. I did not think of myself as poor or rich. We did not live extravagantly by any means, but my girls never lacked anything. Today—especially after they have visited Third World countries—they know they are blessed.

There were times when I denied certain requests. Each Christmas, for example, the girls made lists of toys, books, music or clothes they wanted—and my wife and I would determine what was within the holiday budget. The girls never begged for anything lavish, but there were times when one of them would crawl up into my lap and act exceptionally sweet. I knew a "special request" was coming—especially when they offered unique incentives ("I'll clean my room every day!" for example). And in most cases, I threw the family budget out the window and gave in.

This happened when my oldest daughter, Margaret, was planning her wedding to our first son-in-law, Rick. I had explained to Margaret that we had to stay within a budget, and she agreed. But months later, I learned from my wife that the budget number had climbed by a thousand dollars. I did not remember agreeing to this new figure. But it became obvious that somewhere in all the hustle and bustle of ordering invitations, finding a caterer and buying a wedding dress, my daughter assumed the budget had been raised based on a comment "someone" made. (I never fully understood who changed the figure!) But Margaret won, and Dad happily gave the extra cash. I have never regretted the decision.

I share this story because many women today struggle to believe their heavenly Father wants to bless them. They may have had a dad who abandoned them at birth, or who walked out on the family when they were young kids. Any child of a deadbeat dad knows that money is usually scarce and Christmas is not an easy season. Some women did not have a dad they could approach with their financial requests. Or they may have had a father who was stingy with money, and his lack of generosity made them feel as if they were a financial burden.

You may actually feel financially crippled because of your upbringing. You may feel the ship of blessing has passed you by and docked in someone else's harbor. But if you struggle in this area, you must learn from the story of Achsah. You must be willing to actually *claim* God's blessings.

Blessed to Be a Blessing

The word *prosperity* is a biblical word (various forms of the word appear in Scripture 124 times) but it has a negative connotation to many Christians today because of the way it has been misused by some religious charlatans. Some misguided Bible teachers have promoted the idea that anyone who follows God will automatically become rich; others, because of their own greed, manipulate certain Bible verses on generosity to coerce people into giving in offerings—just so they can buy mansions, designer clothes or private jets.

Let's set aside those erroneous ideas of the so-called prosperity gospel and focus instead on true, biblical prosperity—which has more to do with quality of life than how much money is in your bank account or what model of car you drive. When Jesus promised us an abundant life (see John 10:10), He was talking about so much more than material possessions.

When we walk in God's blessing, His abundance includes healthy relationships, abiding joy, peaceful sleep, personal fulfillment and—most of all—eternal salvation. Prosperity also includes material blessings, including food, clothes, health care, education and a roof over our heads. Our loving Father wants us to have these things; nothing in the Bible indicates that He wants us to be in poverty (He promises to help those who are if they will call on Him). Systemic poverty in a culture is often the longtime result of generations of sin and disobedience to God's laws.

When God called Abram and Sarai to serve Him, He promised them true prosperity. He said: "I will bless you . . . and so you shall be a blessing" (Genesis 12:2). This is an important principle whenever we talk about the blessing of God. He wants to bless us, and He is always generous when He shares His goodness. But God's blessing is never just for us. He desires to bless us in such a way that His blessings spill over and affect others. This means I do not horde His benefits; I share them. And the more I am willing to share His blessings with others, the more He is willing to lavish those blessings on me. As I get to know Him more, I become a conduit of His love to others.

If you study the principle of generosity in Scripture, you learn that it is one of the foundational principles of God's Kingdom. If we are tightfisted with money, then our hands will be closed when it is time to receive from God; if we close our wallets to the needs of others, our wallets will not be open for God's blessings when they come our way. When we give, God gives back to us. And the measure of our giving (not just of our money but also of our time, energy and love) will determine the measure of blessing that comes to us in return.

I do not know what Caleb's daughter, Achsah, planned to do with her well-watered property in Canaan. She and Othniel may have started a farm, or they may have raised sheep, goats or cattle. With access to so much water, they could have raised olives, dates, pomegranates or wheat. And with those abundant resources they could have become quite wealthy. But I would imagine Achsah did not horde her wealth. Because she was a follower of Jehovah, the God of her fathers, she would have given tithes to the priests of Israel, helped the poor, sheltered immigrants and assisted needy families. This is how Israel became a truly prosperous nation— through personal generosity.

American history is full of stories of generous Christian women who did not hoard the blessings of God. One of them was Martha Berry (1866–1942), one of the most prominent women in the state of Georgia during the first half of the twentieth century. Born into a wealthy Southern family, she inherited a huge estate from her father. She knew the land, situated in the Appalachian foothills near Rome, Georgia, would be worth much in the future, and her father urged her to sell it at the right time. But because of her Christian compassion, she chose to use the land to build a school for illiterate, underprivileged mountain children.

Berry came to be known as "the Sunday lady of Possum Trot" when she formed a small Sunday school for kids in a country church near her home.[1] She painted Scriptures on the walls of the building because she did not have enough Bibles to share with the children. After the ministry grew, she decided to open a live-in school for boys. Eventually, in 1902, she deeded her 83-acre homestead to build The Boys Industrial School. This eventually became Berry College, now considered one of the premier liberal arts schools in the South.

An outspoken Christian (her motto was "Prayer changes things"), Berry was not afraid to ask for financial help in order to build her school. She had many famous supporters during her lifetime, including Theodore Roosevelt, Andrew Carnegie and Ellen Louise Wilson, the wife of Woodrow Wilson. She famously asked automobile magnate Henry Ford for money, and he gave her a small sum to test her inventiveness.[2] She put the money to use and increased it, and he then gave her a gift of $1 million—with which she built a huge Gothic-style dormitory complex that has become an icon on the Berry campus.

Martha Berry could have closed her heart to the needs around her. She could have enjoyed a comfortable life at Oak Hill, the mansion on the south end of the Berry property, and spent her life hosting teas and buying new furnishings. Instead, she chose to be generous—and God gave back to her. Millions of dollars poured into the Berry campus to build classrooms, dining halls, a working dairy and administrative buildings. When she died she left a legacy. The motto of her school was: "Not to be ministered unto, but to minister."

Women throughout the history of Christianity have been channels of God's blessing. The famous Amy Carmichael built homes for orphans and prostitutes in India. Relatively unknown missionary Kaay Gordon raised the funds to build twelve churches and two Bible colleges in the freezing Inuit regions of far-northern Canada. Mother Teresa, the famous Albanian nun, was a poor schoolteacher when she went to India to serve the destitute. Yet at the time of her death in 1997, the organization she started, the Sisters of Charity, was operating 517 missions in one hundred countries, and she had raised hundreds of millions of dollars for humanitarian causes.[3] None of these women started out with personal fortunes like Martha Berry, but in the end they became channels of blessing to help others.

God could do similar things through you. Do you desire to help others? Do you want to feed poor children, rescue girls from sex trafficking, build orphanages, help drug addicts, mentor troubled kids, shelter abused women, provide water for African villages or help start churches in a foreign country? You may have never even considered this a possibility because of your own financial limitations. You may be a single mom with a limited budget, a student with school loans to pay or a widow living on a fixed income. I want to challenge you: Do not underestimate God's ability to bless you. He is looking for people to bless with His resources so they can be properly distributed.

Boldness before God

Achsah's story is a clear reminder that we have been called to a life of faith. God wants to bless us, yes. He has territory that He wants to give us, of course. But we inherit the promises of God by believing that He is good, and that He will answer our requests. To be truly blessed, we must believe.

Boldness is a great virtue, but it does not begin on the battlefield or in the midst of a great conflict. Our boldness must begin in our prayer life. We must wrestle our doubts to the ground and believe that God hears our prayers, and that He will answer. We must obey the command found in Hebrews 4:16: "Let us therefore come boldly unto the throne of grace, that we may obtain mercy, and find grace to help in time of need" (KJV).

Do you detect the attitude of Achsah in this verse? It is actually the attitude of all those who have inherited miraculous answers to prayer—whether it be spiritual revival in a city, the recovery of a sick relative or supernatural provision. In order to obtain God's blessings we must ask in faith. We approach God not in timidity or shame, but with great confidence, knowing that we have been made sons and daughters of the King. He has given us legal right to ask—and He does not want us to limit our requests. He challenges us to ask big! We can ask for the upper and the lower springs!

I will never forget the night I met Freda Lindsay, cofounder of Christ For The Nations Institute in Dallas, Texas. She was 94 at the time, and quite frail, but she came to a meeting on the CFNI campus where I was speaking. During a prayer time after my message, she haltingly approached the altar and I knelt to speak to her. Immediately she began to relate to me how many times she had lain on the floor of her campus apartment to pray when the school was facing a financial crisis.

"I didn't know what to do," she said with a smile. "So I just went to the Lord and told Him about the needs we had. And He always answered."

Born in Canada to poor Russian immigrants, she spent her childhood picking berries in Oregon and then became a maid when she was thirteen so she could help her family pay the bills while she finished high school. She later met Gordon Lindsay, a young Pentecostal minister, and they married in 1937. From that point they began a rewarding ministry together that culminated in 1970 with the formation of Christ For The Nations Institute, a school designed to train young ministers.

Freda had gotten her own theological education from a school associated with the Foursquare denomination, and she always shared ministry responsibilities with her husband. But she did not feel prepared for the tragedy that struck on April 1, 1973, when Gordon had a heart attack and died just as a meeting was beginning in the new CFNI student auditorium. Suddenly Freda was thrust into the position of leading a national ministry with huge financial obligations. To make matters worse, some supporters of the ministry demanded that she resign because she was female.

It was during those dark days that Freda learned to come boldly before God's throne. Freda stormed the gates of heaven with her requests, and within eleven months of Gordon's death, supporters had given $83,000 to pay off the CFNI headquarters building. During her many years as president of the school she oversaw the building of numerous dormitories, a student center, a chapel and an athletic field. And until 1994, when she fully turned the leadership of the school over to her son, Dennis, she oversaw the training of thousands of Bible school students, helped plant churches all over the world and assisted hundreds of missionaries.

How did she do these things? It was not through her training (Bible colleges rarely teach people how to pray for money), nor was it because of her administrative skills. But somewhere along the way Freda Lindsay developed the faith of Achsah. She learned to approach God boldly and to ask big. She did not just ask for land; she asked for land and a spring. She grabbed hold of her Father and did not let go until He blessed her with a double portion.

God has the same kind of adventure for you. If you will learn to approach Him with confidence, and believe that your Father longs to give you the Kingdom, you, too, can become a channel of blessing that will affect many.

―――――――― LET'S TALK ABOUT IT ――――――――

1. What impresses you most about Caleb's and his daughter Achsah's faith? How do their lives inspire you?
2. How would you define *prosperity*? Is it only about material possessions?
3. If someone gave you a million dollars, what would you do with it? Do you have a dream to help others that will require a lot of money? Share that dream with your group.
4. When you approach God in prayer, are you bold to ask Him to meet your needs and the needs of others? Or do you hesitate to claim His blessings?

―――――― A MESSAGE FROM YOUR HEAVENLY FATHER ――――――

My precious daughter,

I want to bless you and make you a blessing. If you are struggling financially, come to Me with your anxieties and fears. My Word is clear: If you seek Me first, and My Kingdom, I will add all other things to you. You don't have to worry about food or clothes or material needs. Trust Me and I will provide. When you are worried, come boldly before My throne and ask with confidence. I will not deny you. Do you believe that I am for you? Do you believe that I want to give you all the resources you need to reach others with My love? As you learn to trust Me, I will cause My blessings to overflow in your life so that they touch many. Let Me use you as a conduit for My love, My healing and My provision.

5

Hannah, Mother of Samuel

The Courage to Believe God

> When a train goes through a tunnel and it gets
> dark, you don't throw away the ticket and jump
> off. You sit still and trust the engineer.
>> —Corrie ten Boom (1892–1983),
>> Dutch evangelist and author

Nobody can accomplish great things for God without faith. In fact, Hebrews 11:6 says that without faith it is impossible to please God. History has been written by people who dared to believe God to accomplish the impossible—and usually they overcame overwhelming personal obstacles to reach their goals.

This was true of Irish missionary Amy Carmichael (1867–1951), who dared to establish an orphanage for girls in India at a time when women in that country were treated worse than animals. Amy struggled with chronic neuralgia (she was often bedridden for weeks), and her poor health is the reason the China Inland Mission rejected her as a missionary candidate in 1892. Yet she heard the Lord speak audibly to her and say, "Go ye." She had to look up the phrase in the Bible to understand what it meant. She could not ignore the call.

Amy felt so compelled to touch nations that she ended up spending 55 years in India. She trusted God to provide the funds to care for more than one thousand children at Dohnavur Fellowship, the mission she built in the Tamil Nadu region of India. Her legacy of faith has inspired generations of missionaries—including Elisabeth Elliot, who spent several years reaching Quechua Indians in the jungles of Ecuador after her husband, Jim, was killed in 1956 by a Quechua warrior.

Elisabeth found great encouragement in the prolific writings of Amy Carmichael; she admits to having two shelves of Carmichael's books in her study. She found particular strength in these words from Amy, which capture the intense faith struggle all missionaries face:

> I would never urge one to come to the heathen unless he felt the burden for souls and the Master's call, but oh! I wonder so few do. It does cost something. Satan is tenfold more of a reality to me today than he was in England, and very keenly that awful home-longing cuts through and through one sometimes—but there is a deep joy in being here with Jesus. Praising helps more than anything. Sometimes the temptation is to give way and go in for a regular spell of homesickness and be of no good to anybody. Then you feel the home prayers, and they help you to begin straight off and sing, "Glory, glory, Hallelujah," and you find your cup is ready to overflow again after all.[1]

What would compel a woman like Amy Carmichael to leave the comforts of the Irish countryside and spend most of her life fighting child prostitution in a hostile country where she rarely felt welcome? What would drive a person like Elisabeth Elliot to go to a hostile jungle to tell the people who killed her husband about Christ's love? The answer, of course, is supernatural faith.

Anyone who has ever doubted that God uses women in strategic ways to accomplish His purposes should reread the story of Hannah, the mother of Samuel. She is a true faith hero—a woman who believed God without compromise in a time when Israel was backslidden. Her circumstances were bleak, and most people in her situation would have caved in and given up hope. But Hannah's barren womb and discouraging environment did not stop her. She prayed and believed, then prayed and believed again. In the end, her triumphant prayer of victory is recorded in Scripture—making her one of only a few females who contributed to the writing of the Old Testament.

When we first are introduced to Hannah (whose name means "grace") in 1 Samuel 1, we are told she longed to have a child even though she was barren. I do not believe Hannah's desire was simply a maternal one. This is not the story of a woman who wants to hold an infant in her arms so she can feel good about herself; she did not want a baby so she could push him around in a stroller and prove to the neighbors that she was fertile. On the contrary, Hannah wanted a baby because she was concerned about the lax spiritual condition of her nation.

The narrative about Hannah mentions that Eli was the Lord's priest at the time, and that his sons, Hophni and Phinehas, were conducting the priestly duties in Shiloh. We later learn that Eli's sons were in rebellion against God—they were greedily mishandling the people's offerings and committing sexual immorality in the Lord's house (see 1 Samuel 2:12–17, 22–25). Their behavior shows us that Israel was in a state of moral decay. Hannah was a woman of prayer who was wrestling for the soul of her country. She was praying for a baby because she wanted the Lord to birth an answer to Israel's problems. She wanted her child to grow up and be the Lord's prophet.

When God chooses to use men and women in a significant way, as He used Hannah, He does not allow them to trust in their own abilities. He makes their tasks impossible so that when the supernatural answer comes, only God gets the credit. In Hannah's case, God closed in on her. The Bible says it was the Lord who closed her womb (see 1 Samuel 1:6). He did not close it for good—but He caused her natural ability to shut down so He could reopen it at the proper time. And He placed Hannah in a difficult environment so He could shape her faith for a special task.

Tune Out the Wrong Voices

Besides Hannah's barrenness, there were three negative voices working against her prior to the miraculous birth of Samuel. In my ministry to women around the world, I have seen these same voices working to discourage women and to talk them out of their promises. And I have learned that we must tune out these voices if we expect to receive God's promises.

1. The Voice of Criticism

Hannah's husband, Elkanah, had a second wife, and she was not a pleasant housemate. Can you imagine getting up each morning, going into your kitchen to fix breakfast, and meeting your husband's *other wife*—who has several children? We are told that Elkanah's second wife, Peninnah, taunted Hannah constantly in order to irritate her and make her feel inferior (see 1 Samuel 1:6).

Remember that in Old Testament times women were valued only by their attachment to men. This explains why women were willing to enter polygamous marriages. To them, having to share a husband with one, two, four or six women was better than having no husband at all.

I have ministered to women in cultures where polygamy is still acceptable behavior. When I led a women's conference in Uganda in 2010, for example, some of the women who attended the event grew up in homes with fathers who had as many as eight wives! In some African cultures, men consider multiple wives to be a sign of prosperity and personal power.

Peninnah's name means "coral." She may have been beautiful, like the colorful coral formations in the sea, but like coral she was dangerous. Any deep-sea diver will tell you that if you get near coral, you may end up a bloody mess. Peninnah's words cut like that. Her condemnation and taunting were faith killers. She chided Hannah every day: "Look at me! I have kids! You don't have any! Nah, nah, nah! You'll never have children! God has forgotten you!"

You may not be in a polygamous marriage, but there are many Peninnahs screaming in your ears nonetheless. Many of these voices are in the media. Fashion magazines, advertising campaigns, television shows, movies and music tell women that they are valuable only because of their appearance or sex appeal. These voices are saying: "You're fat. You're ugly. You're stupid. You have nothing to contribute. You don't have the body, the beauty, the brains or the talent to compete. You will never succeed. You might as well give up."

You may even have an actual Peninnah in your life—a woman who criticizes you constantly. I have prayed with women who told me that their mothers, sisters and even church friends fell into this category. Some women are toxic! They speak nothing but critical words. They do not want you to fulfill your God-given destiny.

Hannah was able to press beyond the voice of criticism. She did not allow Peninnah's hateful words to wound her fatally. She tuned out the words of criticism and believed God. You must do the same.

2. The Voice of Compromise

The Bible tells us that Hannah struggled year after year in her barrenness, constantly tormented by Peninnah. Then Elkanah showed up in 1 Samuel 1:8, seemingly to rescue her from her sadness: "Elkanah her husband said to her, 'Hannah, why do you weep and why do you not eat and why is your heart sad? Am I not better to you than ten sons?'"

We have already been told that Elkanah loved Hannah; he showed favoritism to her by giving her a double portion when he served the meal during the harvest festival (see 1 Samuel 1:5). He seemed quite compassionate when he consoled his wife. I am sure he did love her, but let's remember that this man had two wives. He could not give himself fully to Hannah in intimacy because Peninnah was close by.

There is a faint hint of patronizing when Elkanah suggests to his wife that he is "worth more than ten sons." He is actually saying: "Hannah, why don't you give up on your desire for a baby? Quit praying. Leave all that spiritual stuff behind. Just be satisfied with me! Let me be the center of your universe!"

Many Christian women who carry a strong call of God on their lives have been tricked into selling out because of a man. I have met young women who were called to preach or who had the spiritual graces necessary to lead ministries or launch careers. Yet because of pressure from family, culture or peers, they worried that they might not find the right man soon enough—and they decided to marry the first guy who came along, even though he did not have Christian convictions or strong moral character. In the end, these women were not able to fulfill their deepest dreams because they settled for a poor choice in a husband.

Marriage is wonderful, and it is God's plan for many men and women. But no man, no matter how handsome, charming, smart or wealthy, will be able to fulfill you at your deepest core. Only

Christ can do that. This is why it is fruitless to try to fulfill your deepest spiritual desires through a dating or marriage relationship.

Hannah no doubt loved her husband, but we can be grateful that she did not heed his counsel. She continued to pray for the desire of her heart. She continued to intercede for the child she believed God would give her. She did not compromise, even though her husband advised her to do so.

3. *The Voice of Religious Condemnation*

It was one thing to be criticized and patronized at home. But the saddest scene in Hannah's story occurred when she went to God's house at Shiloh and approached the altar. She went there to spend time with the Lord, and you would expect her to be affirmed by the Lord's ministers. But this is not what happened. As Hannah wept bitterly before the Lord, praying for a son and dedicating him to God's service, Eli the priest listened to her from his seat near the doorpost of the Temple. First Samuel 1:12–17 says:

> Now it came about, as she continued praying before the LORD, that Eli was watching her mouth. As for Hannah, she was speaking in her heart, only her lips were moving, but her voice was not heard. So Eli thought she was drunk. Then Eli said to her, "How long will you make yourself drunk? Put away your wine from you." But Hannah replied, "No, my lord, I am a woman oppressed in spirit; I have drunk neither wine nor strong drink, but I have poured out my soul before the LORD. Do not consider your maidservant as a worthless woman, for I have spoken until now out of my great concern and provocation." Then Eli answered and said, "Go in peace; and may the God of Israel grant your petition that you have asked of Him."

Hannah was experiencing the depths of spiritual anguish in prayer. In an Old Covenant sense, she was entering into what the apostle Paul would call *travail*. Before any miraculous answer to prayer, there is always a spiritual birthing process. In Hannah's case, the one person who should have understood her burden—and should have encouraged her to pursue her promise—mocked her. Eli did not discern what God was doing with Hannah. The man in charge of God's house was spiritually clueless.

Sadly, this still happens today. Many of God's ministers do not recognize the grace that is resting on the women who come to them for counsel and encouragement. They may have adopted doctrinal traditions that limit women's involvement in ministry, or they may actually harbor chauvinistic, antiwoman attitudes. The result is tragic.

I met a woman in Missouri several years ago who was in her sixties. She had become a Christian in her early twenties, and at that time she was so in love with the Lord that she spent all her spare time reading the Bible and learning about the Gospel. She was so excited about Jesus, in fact, that she began to sense that she was called to be an evangelist. Finally, she went to her pastor to share the news. She expected him to be excited, and she hoped he would point her in the right direction so she could be trained.

The pastor offered no instruction or encouragement. In fact, he laughed at her! "You are misinformed," the pastor told her. "Women cannot be evangelists. God would never call you to do that. Go home and stop thinking that way." The woman felt crushed, but she obeyed her pastor and let go of her dream. For more than forty years she assumed that God did not place that burden on her heart. When she attended one of my conferences in 2003, she realized she had been misled.

What happened to this woman was like a spiritual abortion. Her dream was killed because a minister spoke words of death—when it actually was his responsibility to mentor and train her in her calling. How many ministers will have to give an account before God because they butchered a promise that was growing inside of one of the Lord's daughters?

If you have a promise growing inside of you, and you know it is from the Lord, you must nurture it in faith. Do not listen to the voices that want to destroy it. Stop listening to the criticism of Peninnah. Do not cave in to the smooth-sounding voice of compromise. And do not allow religious condemnation to kill your dream—no matter what any minister has said to you.

If God has placed a big dream in your heart, He will require you to inherit your promise by faith. There is no other way to birth God's plans in the earth. Regardless of your dream—to see your children return to God, to see a church revitalized, to launch a ministry to street kids, or whatever your heart burns for—you must believe God and be willing to wait for His answer.

Hannah's School of Perseverance

Whenever God wants to bring a Samuel into the world, He looks for a Hannah who is willing to travail. Hannah's waiting period was much longer than a normal gestation period. She prayed desperately for years, and she never gave up hope.

You may have prayed for something for years, and then you woke up one day, breathed a big sigh and said to yourself: *This is crazy. Nothing is happening. God must not be listening.*

If this has been your experience you are not alone. You have been enrolled in the School of Persevering Prayer, and it is not a one-semester class. It is a lifelong journey designed to stretch your faith, develop your character, purify your motives, test your patience and increase your capacity to know and experience God's amazing love.

I have been in this class for a long time, and I do not always make the grade. I often whine about God's delays. For years I brought the same request to the Lord, yet the answer seemed impossibly distant. My faith wavered from calm assurance to frustrated doubt. In my weakest moments I panicked.

There is no way around the fact that prayer requires persistence. Jesus told a parable about an unrighteous judge who granted a poor widow's petition because she badgered him (see Luke 18:1–8). Jesus asked: "Will not God bring about justice for His elect who cry to Him day and night?" (verse 7).

Most people in the Bible who asked God for big things waited a long time to receive their answers. Abraham turned gray waiting for his promised heir—and he is the father of our faith. Joshua and his remnant company wandered in the wilderness forty years before they possessed Canaan. Hannah endured Peninnah's taunts for years. Prayer is not magic. It is a process. When God gives you a promise, you essentially become pregnant with it. If you plan to carry the promise to full term, you must travail.

Surely this is what the apostle Paul experienced when he told the Galatians he would be "in labor" until Christ was formed in them (Galatians 4:19). We often think of the prayer of faith as triggering instant answers, but this was not the case with Paul, nor with Hannah. While God can certainly answer immediately, even with fire from heaven, frequently He calls us to carry a promise until we are mature enough to handle the answer.

Jesus said: "For everyone who asks receives, and he who seeks finds, and to him who knocks it will be opened" (Matthew 7:8). The verbs used are Greek present imperatives, meaning *constant asking, seeking* and *knocking*. Prevailing prayer requires persistence, but when we feel too weak to press forward in faith the Spirit provides the extra push.

Keep on knocking. Never give up. You are closer than ever to a breakthrough.

Every one of us is on a journey of faith, and yours is different from mine because of what God has called each of us to do. But you will find these guidelines helpful as you birth your promise:

1. *Renounce your doubts.* Do not listen to negative voices—especially the ones that play inside your own head. If we are not careful we can fall into the trap of double-mindedness. We say we want to go to our Promised Land, but we hesitate—and all such foot-dragging is doubt. We say we want to go forward, but we are like a moving car that has its parking brake engaged. Faith requires you to release the brake. James warns the double-minded person: "That man ought not to expect that he will receive anything from the Lord" (James 1:7). Doubt will stop you from shifting forward.

2. *Welcome those God sends to help you.* God uses people to push us to the next level. The Body of Christ has many members, and those who are gifted as prophets, intercessors, wise counselors and encouragers will always show up when you are in strategic moments in your faith journey.

   When Moses was weary of the battle and could barely find the strength to pray, God sent Aaron and Hur to lift up his arms (see Exodus 17:12). When Hezekiah was overwhelmed by the threat of Sennacherib's armies, Isaiah brought a word from the Lord that ignited faith for a miraculous victory (see 2 Kings 19). When Mary was perplexed by the daunting task of carrying the Messiah in her womb, Elizabeth released a prophetic blessing over her (see Luke 1:41–45).

   Intercessors who are empowered by the Holy Spirit are like spiritual midwives who help us birth God's promise when we do not have the strength to deliver. Prayer is a painful process, but certain people have an unusual grace from God to travail with us. Allow them to pray for you and speak into your situation.

3. *Contend for your promise.* The enemy is a thief, and he wants to rob us of our inheritance. He does not want us to move forward in God, take new territory, assume new authority or advance into our spiritual callings. Satan is also an abortionist—he wants to devour your promise before it is born.

This is why we must wield God's promise as a weapon against our enemy. Paul wrote: "This command I entrust to you, Timothy, my son, in accordance with the prophecies previously made concerning you, that by them you fight the good fight" (1 Timothy 1:18). God gives us prophetic promises to pull us literally into our future. Declare them over your life, even when the darkness of discouragement is smothering you. God's Word will break satanic resistance.

After Hannah gave birth to Samuel, she launched into a song of praise to the God who had heard her prayer. Her poetic psalm is often compared to the Magnificat, the song of the virgin Mary recorded in Luke 1:46–55. The tone of Hannah's song is confident and forceful. Her mourning has been turned into dancing. The woman who was abused verbally by Peninnah has passed every test, and she has emerged victorious.

She declares in 1 Samuel 2:7–8:

> "The LORD makes poor and rich; He brings low, He also exalts. He raises the poor from the dust, He lifts the needy from the ash heap to make them sit with nobles, and inherit a seat of honor; for the pillars of the earth are the LORD's, and He set the world on them."

It may sound as if Hannah burst on the scene with newfound optimism after God heard her cry and answered her prayer, but

I do not believe that is the case. I believe that she prayed boldly and confidently even in her weakest moments. Even when she was most desperate, and feeling the most barren, she prayed that God would lift her up from the ash heap and use her life to change her nation. In the end, her song was a final remix of all the prayers she had been praying for years.

It will be the same for you. Do not wait until God answers to believe. Ask in faith without doubting, and fight fiercely for your answer. God will reward those who trust Him.

LET'S TALK ABOUT IT

1. God placed a special burden on Hannah to give birth to a baby so that God could change her nation. Do you have a special desire to be used by God? Or do you have a special promise that God has given you that has not yet been fulfilled? Share your dream with the group.
2. Hannah faced three difficult voices in her life: (1) criticism, (2) compromise and (3) religious condemnation. Have you experienced similar opposition as you have tried to serve the Lord?
3. How long have you believed that God will fulfill His promise?
4. The process of inheriting a promise from God is often compared to childbirth in Scripture. How is the Holy Spirit involved in this process?

A MESSAGE FROM YOUR HEAVENLY FATHER

My precious daughter,

I have called you to be a woman of faith. I want to birth My promises in you. My power is not limited by your circumstances, no matter how difficult they may seem. Don't be swayed by what you see around you. I have called you to walk by faith and not by sight. When you hear negative voices of criticism, meditate on My Word. Believe what I have said. Don't let anyone talk you out of My promises. I have given them to you! Don't let the words of men stop you. Build your life on My Word, confess My Word and believe My Word at all times. You are in a battle of faith, but if you trust in Me you will not be disappointed. Though the vision tarries, wait for it. I will birth My promise in you at the appointed time.

6

Esther, Queen of Persia

The Courage to Challenge Injustice

If I could have convinced more slaves that they
were slaves, I could have freed thousands more.

—Abolitionist leader
Harriet Tubman (1820–1913),
founder of the Underground Railroad movement

It is the kind of story that would make a great movie. A frightened orphan girl in ancient Persia is drafted into the harem of King Xerxes (also called Ahasuerus) and is suddenly made his wife. After learning of a plot against the exiled Jews in the land, she risks her life to expose the conspiracy. Because of her bravery, her people are saved from genocide, and her cousin Mordecai, who supported her efforts and inspired her courage, is elevated to serve alongside the heroic young queen.

Unfortunately, *One Night with the King*, the 2006 film about Esther, missed the point entirely. The film turned what should have been a suspenseful drama into a sentimental palace romance. The producers spent $20 million on gorgeous sets, period costumes, special effects and Hollywood actors. But in the end the lavish epic was spoiled because the screenwriter turned a gritty true story into vapid historical fiction.

Young Jewish girls living as exiles in ancient Persia were not thrilled at the prospect of being sexual slaves in the king's palace, and the real Esther would never have danced merrily in Xerxes' courtyard as she awaited her debut in his royal bedchamber. The idea that Esther was goo-goo-eyed over Xerxes is laughable on the surface and insulting to women on a much deeper level.

In the movie, King Xerxes is portrayed as a handsome young guy with long hair who likes to show off his chiseled chest. He seems smitten with Esther after he meets her, and coos over her at the royal wedding.

Xerxes, in reality, was a depraved despot who had dozens of concubines at his disposal. He castrated the men who served in his court, and ruled his kingdom with threats of execution. The real Esther lived under a constant death sentence. The reason she is an Old Testament hero is that she faced unspeakable horror with remarkable faith.

The book of Esther is not about an ancient beauty contest, and it should not be trivialized as a romance. On the contrary, it depicts the brutality and exploitation women have faced through the centuries. It also offers hope to women by spotlighting how God used a brave Jewish girl to challenge the most sinister injustice. It a powerful reminder that God wants to use women to be His dangerous weapons in the struggle against evil.

Rare Courage

Esther's remarkable story is a tale of partnership between her and her cousin, Mordecai, who discovered that the wicked Haman, a henchman of King Xerxes, was scheming to destroy the Jewish settlers in Persia. After Esther was taken by force into the king's harem, Mordecai learned of Haman's genocide plot and sent this famous message to her, recorded in Esther 4:13–14:

> "Do not imagine that you in the king's palace can escape any more than all the Jews. For if you remain silent at this time, relief and deliverance will arise for the Jews from another place and you and your father's house will perish. And who knows whether you have not attained royalty for such a time as this?"

The backdrop of the story is fascinating: Haman, a descendant of Amalekite King Agag, represents the age-old conflict between God's chosen people and the evil forces that hate Him. Motivated by Satan himself, Haman was bent on destroying the righteous seed that would eventually produce the Messiah. Esther and Mordecai, representing the righteous remnant of those who love the true God, were called upon to join forces and oppose this demonic attack. To do so, they both had to risk their lives and trust God to deliver them and their persecuted people.

It is clear throughout the story that God sovereignly chose to use both Mordecai *and* Esther in His rescue plan. Esther could not have exposed Haman's plot without the information she received from her cousin, nor without his prodding; likewise, Mordecai could not have delivered his people if Esther had not worked as a palace "insider." In the end, after Esther exposed Haman's scheme and he was executed, both she and Mordecai were given unprecedented authority in the kingdom.

The message is not subtle: God uses both male and female to accomplish His purposes on earth. Men do not run the show by themselves.

But Esther was not a Superwoman figure. She did not wear a cape or possess superpowers. She was actually a shy girl, most likely terrified at the prospect of sleeping with a powerful man who could order her death at any moment. When she first learned of Haman's plot, the Bible says she "writhed in great anguish" (Esther 4:4), and then she tried to convince Mordecai to take off his sackcloth so that he would not draw attention. Her first reaction was to pretend the problem was not real.

But when it became clear that Mordecai was serious about opposing Haman, and that she must speak with the king urgently, she woke up and faced reality. She chose to steel her nerves and put her fears aside. She sent this message to her cousin, recorded in Esther 4:16:

> "Go, assemble all the Jews who are found in Susa, and fast for me; do not eat or drink for three days, night or day. I and my maidens also will fast in the same way. And thus I will go in to the king, which is not according to the law; and if I perish, I perish."

Esther did not rely on her own strength. She called on God, and she asked others to mobilize prayer on her behalf. She knew she was sunk if God did not answer. She was terrified, but this did not stop her from doing what was right. Great faith often emerges out of desperation and anguish, and people who perform brave deeds always battle fears of failure and defeat.

In the end, Esther's love for her people, and for the God who had protected Israel through the ages, compelled her to run to the front lines of the battle instead of cowering behind the palace curtains or under its pillows. Because of her remarkable courage, she and Mordecai ended up changing the law of the land.

Many Christian women over the centuries have displayed similar courage in the face of evil. One of the best examples is Mary Slessor (1848–1915), a short, redheaded Presbyterian missionary from Scotland who became known as "The White Ma" in the region of Nigeria where she preached and ministered for 39 years. The daughter of an alcoholic father, Slessor worked in a cotton mill and was told she could not preach because she was a woman. But her passion for missions drove her on, and she found special inspiration from the life of David Livingston—the British explorer who carved out trails into the interior of Africa so missionaries could reach its people.[1]

Livingston was Slessor's Mordecai. When he died in 1873, she felt she must continue his drive to reach Africa for Christ. She was determined to go "where no other white person has settled." She eventually sailed to West Africa, at age 28, and single-handedly established a base of operations in the Calabar region, a dangerous area where traditional rulers worshiped demons, killed babies and buried widows alive in their husband's graves.

Ever spunky and defiant in the face of ignorance, injustice and malaria (she battled the disease often), Slessor was known to preach directly to tribal kings—challenging their mistreatment of women and children. She is best known for opposing the horrific practice of killing twins (local superstition said twins were an evil omen), and she convinced locals to dismantle this tradition. Today in modern Nigeria, Slessor is honored as a spiritual mother who not only saved the lives of children and women but who ignited the fires of spiritual revival that still burn in that nation.[2]

This same compelling boldness convinced an Australian grandmother, Irene Gleeson, to sell her beachfront home near Sydney in 1991 so she could move to Africa. At 47, Gleeson had planned to retire and play with her thirteen grandchildren, but she could not stop thinking about the plight of children in northern Uganda who were being exploited and killed by the terrorist group known as the Lord's Resistance Army (LRA).

This brave Pentecostal woman sold her home and used the money to fund her move to one of the most dangerous places on earth. Aid organizations told her she was naïve for thinking she could set up camp in Uganda; missions groups advised her to go to Bible college instead; friends suggested she minister in safer places. Instead, Gleeson flew to Kampala, Uganda's capital, and took a bus as far as it would go into enemy territory. She finally reached Kitgum, a desolate town located forty miles south of the Sudan border. The first thing she saw was a woman afflicted with polio who was crawling on the ground like a spider.

Gleeson told *Charisma* magazine that when she saw the twisted woman, and the desperate poverty and the condition of the children, she said to herself: "I will help these people, no matter how hard it gets."[3] She found a big tree and began to teach Bible lessons to children under its shade. God sent money from all over the world to fund her mission.

Today, the ministry Gleeson founded, Childcare Kitgum Servants, assists more than eight thousand children daily. It operates three primary schools, a vocational training center, a hospice for AIDS victims, a church and a radio station that blasts the Gospel to one million people living in a region that has been torn apart by genocide. She has been threatened often. LRA soldiers once mashed her arm with a stick and held an AK–47 rifle in her face, but she brandished her best weapon by rebuking the men in the name of Jesus. They eventually fled.

Embrace Esther's Process

As a result of Gleeson's bravery, hundreds of children who would have been forced to become LRA soldiers have instead graduated from school, learned professions and even become pastors. One boy named Francis, who was regularly beaten by the local witch doctor, became the founder of a seven-hundred-member church.

Why do we not see more Mary Slessors and Irene Gleesons rising up today to fight darkness? I am convinced that fear is the key reason. It certainly is not because there are no Hamans plotting to kill today. Our world is a dangerous place, whether because of infanticide, sexual abuse, sex trafficking, mistreatment of widows and orphans, child abandonment or sex-selective abortion. According to Nobel Prize laureate Dr. Amartya Sen, approximately one hundred million women are "missing" worldwide because of female infanticide or mistreatment.

In India, where boys are favored over girls—and some women kill their girl babies because they cannot afford to pay their dowry at marriage time—there are only 900 women to every 1,000 men. In the Indian states of Bihar and Rajasthan, the female-male ratio is a startling 600 to 1,000.[4]

The statistics regarding organized sex trafficking and child slavery are equally as frightening. The United Nations estimates that 2.5 million people are enslaved today; this includes young children working fourteen-hour shifts in brick kilns in Pakistan, and fourteen-year-old Vietnamese girls who are drugged and forced to work as prostitutes until they contract the AIDS virus. A report from the United Nations states that 98 percent of sex trafficking victims are women and girls, and 95 percent of them suffer physical or sexual violence.[5]

Statistics like these rarely move people to action. But when we see a face, interview a victim in person or see photos of the atrocities going on all around us, we are more likely to step in and help. This happened to me in 2012 when, during my second trip to Uganda, I saw documentation of what is happening to twelve-year-old girls in the eastern regions of the country. There, because of tribal traditions, girls are rounded up and forced to endure the cruel practice of female genital mutilation (FGM).

Many of the girls are tied with ropes to prevent them from escaping; then, an untrained "surgeon" uses a common knife to remove the clitoris and outer labia of the girls' sex organs. Those supervising this barbaric ritual do not respond to the girls' screams, nor do they offer any lasting pain relief. Most tribal leaders in eastern Uganda condone FGM because they believe it will teach the girls not to engage in sexual immorality.

After I saw photos and statistics about this problem, I decided to act. I immediately began working to empower local Christians to begin an educational campaign designed to stop this practice, so that Ugandan girls can grow up without the pain and shame of mutilation and the diseases and infections that accompany it.

Let me ask you: Is God calling you to expose one of Haman's plots? Has the Holy Spirit burdened you to confront some form of injustice? Do not fall for the familiar lie that says you cannot change a social problem because you are "just one person." Esther was a seemingly insignificant young woman with no pedigree and no funding, and her racial background made her an outcast. Yet because of God's favor on her life, she was elevated into position to change history. God can do the same with you if you are willing to embrace a similar process. Esther took these steps:

1. *She died to her desires.* When Esther was taken into the palace, she was required to submit to two six-month treatments of myrrh and spices. These were most likely to soften her skin and make her as beautiful as possible for the king's expensive tastes. But whenever we see myrrh and spices mentioned in Scripture, this also has a deeper spiritual connotation.

Myrrh was presented to Jesus at His birth; the women who followed Him brought it to His tomb. It represents the very fragrance of Christ that works in all true believers who have denied themselves and taken up His cross. We cannot walk in fearless obedience if we have not submitted to the myrrh treatment. We must die to what we want; we must be willing to leave our own comfort and embrace whatever suffering might be required to follow the Master.

2. *She was moved with compassion.* When Mordecai learned of Haman's plan to destroy the Jews, he tore his clothes, put on sackcloth and "wailed loudly and bitterly" (Esther 4:1). He was not putting on an act. Mordecai was genuinely moved with deep concern for his people. No doubt he imparted this same compassion to his spiritual daughter when he raised her.

Initially, because of fear, Esther wanted to silence Mordecai's compassionate cries. But in the end, she was so troubled by the specter of genocide that she agreed to intervene. It was love that moved her. This is the only power that will move us to rescue the perishing. If we do not care, we will not act. But if we open our hearts wide enough to feel what God feels for those who are suffering injustice, love will prod us into action.

3. *She swallowed her fears.* It was C. S. Lewis who said: "Courage is not simply one of the virtues, but the form of every virtue at the testing point."[6] Ultimately, nothing is accomplished for God without courage, because without it we will always quit before trying. Esther was backed into a dark corner, and she could easily have taken the more convenient path of self-preservation. Yet God gave her the boldness to look murder in the eyes and expose it, even though she knew the king could have sent her to the gallows for discrediting Haman.

4. *She mobilized prayer.* Esther knew she could not tackle this task alone, even though her praying maidens would not be with her when she confronted Haman. She organized a prayer vigil because she understood the power of united intercession. If you choose to attack injustice on any level, you will need the same prayer covering.

Mary Slessor, the missionary to Nigeria, once wrote to a friend who had prayed for her for many years, and stated that it was the prayers of the saints that pushed her to spiritual victory. She said:

> I have always said that I have no idea how or why God has carried me over so many funny and hard places, and made these hordes of people submit to me, or why the government should have given me the privilege of a magistrate among them, except in answer to prayer made at home for me. It is all beyond my comprehension. The only way I can explain it is on the ground that I have been prayed for more than most. Pray on, dear one—the power lies that way.[7]

Do not cave in to intimidation. You can fight injustice. Just as Esther did, you can stare fear in the face, point your finger at it and overthrow it.

Let's Talk about It

1. Explain why the story of Esther should not be romanticized. In what ways did Esther display uncommon courage?
2. Mordecai and Esther were partners in their struggle against the wicked plans of Haman. How does this reveal God's plan for men and women?
3. Missionaries such as Mary Slessor and Irene Gleeson engaged in brave efforts to oppose injustice. Do you feel prompted to engage in fighting certain social evils? How can you do this?

4. Esther swallowed her fears and died to her own desires before
she engaged the enemy. What fears or self-centered attitudes
might stand in the way of your becoming a fearless woman?

——— A MESSAGE FROM YOUR HEAVENLY FATHER ———

My precious daughter,

*Like Esther, I have adopted you and made you a part of
My family. You can be secure in My love—and in that security
you can walk in supernatural boldness. There is an enemy
who wants to devour and destroy people, but I have empowered you to expose and overthrow him. Let Me prepare you.
Don't shrink back from the conflict. Let courage arise in your
heart. Like Esther, I have given you favor to influence others.
You are My secret weapon! Don't be afraid to speak out on
behalf of those who have been sentenced to death. I will be
with you. I will give you the words to say and the courage to
speak. And in the end, I will use you to stop injustice.*

7

Miriam, Sister of Moses

The Courage to Lead in a Man's World

Being powerful is like being a lady. If you have
to tell people you are, you aren't.
—British Prime Minister Margaret Thatcher

ost people think of Moses as one of the greatest leaders in
the Old Testament—a rugged man of courage, and full of
testosterone, who took up God's rod of authority and challenged
Pharaoh to liberate the Hebrews from Egyptian bondage. But the
story of the Exodus is not just about man's accomplishments. It is
laced with estrogen as well. It began when several fearless women
paved the way for Moses' rise to power.

First, the Hebrew midwives, Shiphrah and Puah, disobeyed
Pharaoh's edict to kill all male babies because they "feared God"
(Exodus 1:17, 21). Second, Moses' mother hid her baby in a water-
proof basket along the reedy banks of the Nile, in another act of

civil disobedience that was punishable by death. Third, Pharaoh's own daughter pulled the baby Moses out of the river and adopted him—and employed Moses' mother to nurse him. In each case, it was a woman who undermined the evil plans of the Egyptian ruler. This is how Moses came to grow up in the house of Pharaoh. None of this could have happened without the women who scurried in the background to carry out God's sovereign will in the face of danger.

But our focus here turns to another woman in the story, Moses' sister, Miriam, whom we first meet when she was just a girl watching her baby brother from a safe distance, his basket afloat in the Nile (see Exodus 2:4). Even at a young age Miriam served as a protector. When Pharaoh's daughter pulled the infant out of the crude basket and realized he was a Hebrew, Miriam ran from her hiding place and volunteered to help. Exodus 2:7 says: "Then his sister said to Pharaoh's daughter, 'Shall I go and call a nurse for you from the Hebrew women that she may nurse the child for you?'"

These were not the words of a shy girl. Slaves do not just run into the presence of royalty and start chattering. Miriam was different. She had been raised in a house full of faith, and her parents had obviously instilled unusual confidence in her. She did some fast thinking on her feet when she suggested that "a nurse" (her mother, Jochebed) could nurture the child until he was weaned. Miriam, even in her preteen days, displayed remarkable courage and intelligence, and her intervention not only saved her brother's life but set the stage for Israel's deliverance. Never underestimate the power of a woman to save the day!

The next time we meet Miriam in Scripture is on the shores of another body of water—just after Pharaoh's army was drowned in the Red Sea. She had been with Moses and their brother, Aaron, all along. She had watched as God brought judgment on Egypt with the ten plagues; she had hidden inside her house, with blood on her door, as the angel of death had passed over the Hebrew nation. She had eaten the Passover meal in haste. After the miraculous parting of the Red Sea, Miriam led God's people in praise. Exodus 15:20 says: "Miriam the prophetess, Aaron's sister, took the timbrel in her hand, and all the women went out after her with timbrels and with dancing."

The first time we met Miriam she was a quick-thinking girl; now she is referred to as "a prophetess." She has grown up, and her spiritual gifts have matured. Carrying the designation of prophetess was no small thing—God's hand was on this woman's life and she carried His message. She heard God's voice, and she spoke for Him.

It is interesting that the Bible does not tell us anything about the process Miriam went through to become a leader. One day she was a girl watching over her little brother; the next time we see her she was leading the congregation of Israel. Many years had passed, and many lessons were learned. God prepares His leaders in obscurity, while no one is watching. You may actually feel you are in that place of hiddenness right now, and you may be wondering if God will ever promote you from the shadows into a place of effective ministry. You will not be in the preparation phase forever. Be assured that the sovereign Lord knows exactly where you are, and He will exalt you at the proper time.

Miriam was in a special category of biblical women who were called as spiritual leaders. This is confirmed in Micah 6:4, which says: "Indeed, I brought you up from the land of Egypt and ransomed you from the house of slavery, and I sent before you Moses, Aaron *and Miriam*" (emphasis added).

This passage is significant because it reveals that Miriam was not just a tagalong on the journey through the wilderness. She was not an inferior appendage, smiling from her tent, washing clothes and preparing food with the other women while Moses and Aaron managed the problems of the nomadic nation. Miriam was given authority by God to lead. She functioned, along with her brothers, as a governing elder.

Sadly, because of misinterpretation of Scripture and chauvinistic attitudes, many Christians today do not tend to recognize women who have leadership gifts, and many do not believe God places women in authority, ever. Yet we have clear record here that Miriam was appointed to a place of senior leadership—at a time in history when men ran everything.

A Modern Miriam

If you happen to meet Pastor Indri Gautama in one of the trendy shopping malls in downtown Jakarta, Indonesia, you might be tempted to think she is an investment banker or the president of a multinational corporation. Usually dressed in tailored suits, and never without her cell phone, the petite Chinese woman scurries from one meeting to another. She is constantly sending text messages to her office and talking in rapid-fire Indonesian to the dozens of people who work for her.

But Gautama is not a banker or a businesswoman. Those who know her best call her "Apostle Indri." She is comfortable with the title because she has planted a thriving church movement in the heart of the world's largest Muslim nation.

Gautama was raised in a wealthy Chinese family. Her father's focus was always on money. Her mother had originally planned to abort her. Both parents practiced ancestor worship. After graduating from college in Australia she moved in with a Middle Eastern man in Honolulu and spent much of her time in discos. During that rough period of her life she had seven abortions.

Yet in 1984, after returning to Jakarta, she heard the Gospel and gave her life to Jesus Christ while visiting a dying AIDS patient in a Jakarta hospital.

Despite her penchant for nice suits and designer handbags, she is not a Christian diva. She cut her teeth in the ministry by giving her life for the poor. Early in her ministry she learned the importance of giving in order to break the cycle of financial lack.

In 1993, at age 36, she sold her passport business and a toy factory she owned and gave away her other businesses. She became an itinerant evangelist to the people living on the island of Sulawesi—and then to other dangerous areas where Muslims often burn churches.

Gautama grabbed attention in Jakarta when she began a church in the city in 2002, starting with only seven people. When Gautama founded Apostolic Generation Church she had little training and no support from male pastors in the city, but the congregation began to grow exponentially. Gautama and her members eventually built an impressive downtown complex known as Kuningan Place, which features apartments, offices, a 1,000-seat auditorium, a day-care center and a parking garage, all housed in four skyscrapers, the tallest of which is thirty stories.

When I asked Gautama to describe her vision, she talked rapidly and with passion—just as she does in the pulpit. "The members of my church know that they are called to be His transforming agents," she told me. "We are to win, nurture and disciple souls and develop them to be apostolic leaders so that we can advance the Kingdom of God."[1]

In my ministry travels I have met many women ministers like Indri Gautama who hold positions of senior leadership. Some are pioneer missionaries working in difficult places such as Saudi Arabia, Siberia, Sudan or the mountains of Ecuador. Others are building churches in major metropolitan cities. All seem to have the kiss of God on their labors. Yet when I come back from my trips and look around at the United States, I see that we have precious few women in such positions. Why is this? In my view it stems almost entirely from a distorted view of Scripture.

The Case for Women Leaders

Along with Miriam, the Bible contains numerous examples of godly women who held positions of spiritual authority and influence. The first woman, Eve, was commissioned by God to "fill the earth, and subdue it; and rule" alongside her husband (Genesis 1:28). We have already studied the life of Sarah, who believed with Abraham for the Promised Land. Deborah, a prophet like Miriam, ruled Israel as a judge and rallied the people to victory over their enemies. Huldah, a contemporary of the prophet Jeremiah, counseled King Josiah and foretold coming judgments on the nation. In the New Testament, we find an equal number of women who served in positions of spiritual authority.

Yet despite the clear record of Scripture, many modern fundamentalists and evangelicals tend to ignore these women even while championing a so-called literal approach to the Bible. The truth is that these so-called literalists are actually twisting Scripture. They conveniently ignore the references that endorse women in leadership positions. They might as well take scissors and snip them out of the Bible.

These individuals usually turn to Paul's words in 1 Timothy 2:12 to prove their point: "I do not allow a woman to teach or exercise authority over a man, but to remain quiet." Quoting this verse, they mandate that no woman at any time may assume a position of church leadership. But is this really what the Bible says?

Reading a little further in Paul's letters to Timothy, we see that after this warning about the dangers of female leadership, he praised Timothy's mother and grandmother for laying spiritual foundations in the young man's life: "For I am mindful of the sincere faith within you, which first dwelt in your grandmother Lois and your mother Eunice, and I am sure that it is in you as well" (2 Timothy 1:5).

On the one hand he told women not to teach men; on the other hand he praised women for training Timothy. So how do we interpret these passages? Do Paul's words construct an ironclad prohibition against women in leadership? Is he suggesting that women are allowed to teach other women or children in church settings, but not adult men? But if women are not allowed to teach or lead men, why did God appoint Miriam as a prophetess and leader in ancient Israel?

The "no women in authority" rule is based primarily on these words in 1 Timothy 2:12: *exercise authority over a man*. The King James Version offers a more precise rendering of the Greek text here, stating that Paul did not allow a woman to "usurp authority." Actually, there is no word in the English language to translate *authentein* accurately, although *usurp* is close enough. The Greek verb denotes a violent act with almost murderous connotations.[2]

Most serious Bible scholars believe that Paul was addressing, in 1 Timothy 2, a serious deception that had crept into the primitive Ephesian church. Because the cult of Artemis, a Greek fertility goddess, was headquartered in Ephesus, strange spiritual influences were swirling around the region—including cult prostitution, ritual homosexuality, bizarre ideas about the sexes and a form of goddess worship promoting the idea that Eve was created before Adam and, therefore, superior to him.

Paul was refuting these ideas, as well as clamping down on the false teachers (probably women) who promoted these dangerous, pre-Gnostic doctrines—and his solution was not only to muzzle the women involved, but also to demand that they submit in silence to proper doctrine.

Bible "literalists" who forbid women to hold positions of authority argue, however, that another passage supports their point. They turn to 1 Corinthians 14:34. Here Paul wrote: "The women are to keep silent in the churches." From this they conclude that Paul never allowed women to pray publicly, prophesy, preach or teach anywhere or anytime. Many traditional Christians have made 1 Corinthians 14:34 the primary lens through which to view all women's ministry in the church age. They assume God is pleased when women keep their mouths shut.

This is a laughable concept, especially when you consider that Paul mentioned women prophesying and praying just three chapters earlier in his letter to the Corinthians, and he did not restrict them! (See 1 Corinthians 11:4–16, which addresses cultural issues about how men and women should dress in church.) Actually, Paul affirmed the spiritual gifts of women and encouraged them to become good students of the Word of God.

More than 150 years ago in England, a bold woman preacher named Catherine Booth—cofounder of The Salvation Army with her husband, William—wrote a popular pamphlet defending women ministers. A fiery orator and soul-winner who trained hundreds of women evangelists known as "Hallelujah lassies," Booth tried to convince tradition-bound ministers to make room for women in the pulpits of Britain. She pointed out in *Female Ministry; or, Woman's Right to Preach the Gospel* that the misinterpretation of 1 Corinthians 14:34 is one of the primary reasons why women are wrongly restricted from speaking for God. She wrote:

> There is no end to the errors in faith and practice which have resulted from taking isolated passages, wrested from their proper

116

connections, or the light thrown upon them by other Scriptures, and applying them to sustain a favorite theory. Judging from the blessed results which have almost invariably followed the ministrations of women in the cause of Christ, we fear it will be found, in the great day of account, that a mistaken and unjustifiable application of the passage, "Let your women keep silence in the churches," has resulted in more loss to the church, evil to the world, and dishonor to God, than any of the errors we have already referred to.[3]

Scholars disagree about what Paul was specifically correcting in this passage. It could have been undignified behavior between husbands and wives during corporate teaching sessions, or Paul may have actually included a quote from traditionally minded Jewish-Christian leaders who believed women should be seen and not heard in church.

Regardless of the specific interpretation, Paul the apostle did not believe in universally silencing women. He had too many effective women ministers who were his contemporaries in church leadership to do that, including the Bible teacher Priscilla, who helped plant churches all over the Roman empire with her husband, Aquila (see Romans 16:3–4 and 1 Corinthians 16:19, for example; we will look at Priscilla's ministry in more detail in chapter 15), along with Phoebe, Euodia, Syntyche, Nympha, Persis and Junia.

We must stop viewing the role of women through the narrow filter of Paul's words to Timothy or to the Corinthians. Women speak for God freely throughout the Old and New Testaments; why would we restrict all women based on these injunctions to heretical or immature churchgoers? We cannot use these verses as a blanket rule for all churches in all times.

In addition, we find further enlightenment on this subject in the Bible's teaching on motherly authority. The Scriptures are replete with references to the influence of a woman over her own children. In Proverbs, for instance, a son is warned not to abandon the instruction of his mother. Throughout Scripture, parents are challenged as couples to use discipline, instruction, exhortation and the rod of correction to train their youngsters. And in the New Testament, women whose husbands are not even believers are told that they possess priestly authority to influence their families for righteousness (see 1 Peter 3:1–2).

Also in the New Testament, older women who were godly examples to a congregation were set apart to serve in a special capacity. The word for *older women* in Titus 2:3 is the word *presbytera*, from which we derive the word *presbytery*, or *elder's council*. In the early Church, those who exhibited wisdom and godly character were designated as elders so they could go about "teaching what is good" (Titus 2:3).

God never intended men to nurture the Church alone. Just as He gave each child two parents—a mother and a father—He desires spiritual mothers and fathers to instruct and edify His people. Yet in many tradition-bound churches today where women are restricted, there is no room for spiritual mothers. The message of the Bible has been twisted to suggest that it is never appropriate for a woman to teach or influence a man. We have, therefore, become a motherless people. And as a result we see fewer Timothys emerging.

I believe it is time for the Church to fling open her doors and allow spiritual mothers to take their places on the front lines. We need their wisdom, their passion, their spiritual gifts, their instruction and their correction. Only when they are positioned alongside the men of the Church, as Miriam stood alongside Moses and Aaron, will we truly be able to see the manifest presence and power of God released.

A Word of Caution

Just as the Bible reveals the flaws and failures of leaders such as King David, King Hezekiah and Moses himself, so we see Miriam, warts and all. The account of her public discipline, told in Numbers 12, reminds us that to whom much is given, much is required.

Both Aaron and Miriam "spoke against Moses" because they did not approve of his choice in a wife, and they specifically questioned his ability to hear God. They said: "Has the LORD indeed spoken only through Moses? Has He not spoken through us as well?" (Numbers 12:2). God was not happy about their attack on Moses' character. After a swift rebuke from the cloud of His presence, Miriam was suddenly covered with leprosy (indicating that perhaps she had instigated this argument). Aaron pleaded to Moses for her life, and Moses pleaded to God for her healing. In the end she was healed, but she endured a shameful banishment outside the camp for seven days until they could guarantee she had no trace of the disease.

Why is this story in the Bible? It serves as a warning to anyone in leadership. We must honor delegated spiritual authority and respect our boundaries. Miriam was anointed as a prophetess, and she no doubt heard from God and spoke for Him. But gifted people must be on their guard: The most talented celebrities can become the most arrogant, and this triggers the beginning of a humiliating downfall. People who are gifted to preach, prophesy and represent God must be careful to stay humble, or they will contract and spread the deadly infection of pride.

Notice that God did not kill Miriam—He disciplined her. This is how He deals with His sons and daughters who get out of line. It was Charles Spurgeon who wrote: "No matter how dear you are to God, if pride is harbored in your spirit, He will whip it out of you."[4] God was not against Miriam because she was a woman in leadership; on the contrary, He was intent on correcting her attitudes so that she could be a better leader.

If you as a woman feel called to leadership, you face the same lonely and difficult journey all leaders face. Your motives will be questioned, your decisions will be criticized, and your sermons will be scrutinized. People will flatter you on Sunday and betray you by Friday. Prepare your heart now for the pain. Leadership is a great calling with many rewards, but it requires not only sacrifice but also total death to self. If you walk humbly before God, He will bless you; but if you become puffed up, or think that your spiritual gifts originate from your own abilities, God will surely humble you until your pride is ground into powder.

I have mentored many women leaders over the years, and I caution them to develop these qualities if they intend to finish well:

1. *Servant leadership.* There are few things more disgusting than a leader who loves attention and thinks the ministry is about her. We do not need any more "divas" in the ministry today. The diva is known for her big demands (limousines, big honoraria and royal treatment) and an aura of self-importance. Godly leaders know that they must be broken so that the life of Jesus can flow from them. If we are not willing to lay our lives down for others, we have no business being in ministry.

2. *A gracious spirit.* True leaders are team players, not lone rangers. I have met women in ministry who act like the fearsome fashion publisher from the movie *The Devil Wears Prada.* They are control freaks who run their ministries with iron fists. This may work for people in the corporate world, but it has no place in God's Kingdom. If anger or insecurity is being suppressed in your life, be sure to deal with it before

you step into leadership or you will leave a trail of wounded people everywhere you go.

3. *Sexual purity.* Sadly, there are women in spiritual leadership who, after coming to Christ, have never dealt with their sexual problems. As a result they flirt with men on the job, dress provocatively and make unwise choices in their relationships. A woman who is called to ministry must crucify her lusts and close every door to sexual temptation, or she will end up a casualty when the devil launches his attacks.

4. *Sound doctrine.* Paul clamped down on the women of Ephesus because they were teaching heresy. He supported women like Priscilla and Phoebe because they preached the Word of God. In a time when many Christians are being deceived, we need women who are rooted and grounded in the truth. Do not try to be a freelance preacher. Get the theological training you need, study diligently, read voraciously and be willing to ask others to critique your message so you will never step out of bounds.

5. *A forgiving spirit.* I have met women in church leadership who have what I call a man-hating spirit. They were wounded by men in the past, and they still have not taken their pain to the cross and embraced Christ's healing. They are nursing grudges and harboring bitterness, and the poison spreads to everyone around them. An unhealed person cannot heal others. A woman who claims a position of leadership because it is "her right" is headed on a collision course with the same God who disciplined Miriam after she angrily attacked her brother's authority.

God desires healthy leadership—from both the men and women who are anointed to serve. If you are one of those women, you can trust that He will not only prepare you for your ministry but also give you abundant grace to fulfill it. It begins with the courage to say yes to the call.

Let's Talk about It

1. Miriam is described as a prophetess in Exodus 15:20 and as one of the leaders of Israel in Micah 6:4. Discuss how you view the issue of women in leadership. Do you have any concerns about women in senior positions of authority?
2. Can you think of a woman in leadership you admire? Describe the qualities in her you think are admirable.
3. Why is it so difficult for women to step into positions of spiritual authority today? Have you ever been told you could not be in a leadership position because of your sex?
4. First Timothy 2:12 is often used to prohibit women from teaching, preaching and serving in church leadership. Explain why this passage cannot be used to make a universal ban on women in leadership.
5. Miriam made a serious mistake as a leader, and was disciplined by the Lord for it. What are the most common mistakes women leaders make, in your opinion?

A Message from Your Heavenly Father

My precious daughter,

You have a high calling in Christ Jesus. I made you a woman, but I also placed leadership potential in you. You are not inferior. Whether you are called to lead a church, a business, a small group, a children's program or a neighborhood Bible study, I can empower you with the boldness you need. Don't limit Me and My power in your life. Just as

Miriam grew in confidence and became a prophetess to her nation, so can you grow in your gifts and abilities. Let Me train you. Let Me chisel your character and form Christ in you. Let Me speak through you. Just as I disciplined Miriam as a daughter, I will break, shape, mold and make you into a woman who honors her Father.

8

Deborah, Judge of Israel

The Courage to Fight

> Be an enemy—a fighting enemy of the world,
> the flesh and the devil. Be an aggressor; carry
> the war into the enemy's camp. Be a fighter, a
> soldier, a man or woman who has the fire of war
> against sin in blood and bone.
>
> —Evangeline Booth (1865–1950),
> daughter of William and Catherine Booth
> and the fourth general of The Salvation Army

I have a special place in my heart for the biblical leader Deborah because my wife shares the same name. The Hebrew word actually means "bee"—and the root of the word means "to speak." Jewish writers, who list Deborah as one of the seven prophetesses of the Old Testament (with Sarah, Miriam, Hannah, Abigail, Huldah and Esther), see in her several bee-like qualities, including industriousness, wisdom and sweetness of temper to her friends—and fierceness to her enemies. She was a wise and courageous woman, but she also had quite a sting.

Chances are you have not heard many sermons about Deborah. Even though she figured prominently in the Old Testament as one of Israel's most successful rulers, many modern churchgoers—those who remain bound by misunderstanding Paul's words to Timothy (see 1 Timothy 2:12)—do not know what to do with her. She was a woman, and she was in senior leadership. To complicate matters further, Deborah had a militant side. She does not fit within the traditional Christian grid for a woman, so the tendency is to ignore her or explain her away as a biblical aberration. Some Christians want to apologize for her, as if she stepped out of line when she assumed her authority.

But the Bible does not cast any aspersions on Deborah, either for her leadership role or her feisty spirit. She is introduced plainly and simply as the leader of Israel. Judges 4:4–5 says:

> Now Deborah, a prophetess, the wife of Lappidoth, was judging Israel at that time. She used to sit under the palm tree of Deborah between Ramah and Bethel in the hill country of Ephraim; and the sons of Israel came up to her for judgment.

Deborah called herself "a mother in Israel" (Judges 5:7). She was obviously a wise problem solver and a compassionate leader who rolled up her sleeves to serve her people. Her skills as a judge were matched equally by her courage. The Bible tells us that she summoned Israel's military commander, Barak, and advised him to prepare a militia of ten thousand men. Their enemy, Jabin, king of Canaan, was preparing an attack, and his army far outnumbered Israel's. But because she was a woman of faith who was connected closely to God, she revealed that the Lord would defeat Jabin's commander, Sisera.

Deborah prophesied to Barak that God would give Sisera into his hand, and she assured him victory. But Barak replied in a most curious way. He said, "If you will go with me, then I will go; but if you will not go with me, I will not go" (Judges 4:8). Some traditionalists criticize Barak for this statement, as if it reveals a cowardly spirit. But this cannot be, for two reasons: (1) Barak's victory song, co-authored with Deborah, celebrates his valor on the battlefield; and (2) he is actually honored in the New Testament as a hero of faith (see Hebrews 11:32–33). He was not being a sissy when he said he needed Deborah to be on the battlefield. On the contrary, he was displaying wisdom. He did not want to face the enemy without the Lord's prophet beside him assuring him of supernatural victory.

Deborah replied to Barak that she would indeed go into battle with him. "Nevertheless," she added, "the honor shall not be yours on the journey that you are about to take, for the LORD will sell Sisera into the hands of a woman" (Judges 4:9). This was not a rebuke. Deborah was prophesying about the unique outcome of this battle. She was also underscoring the fact that God has reserved certain victories for his women warriors. (This is a clear message to all male spiritual leaders: If you are willing to empower women in leadership, then prepare yourself for the fact that women will get some of the credit when success occurs!)

Deborah's prophecy was fulfilled to the letter. Sisera's armies were routed and all his soldiers were killed. He fled on foot from the scene, thinking he could hide in the countryside. But as providence would direct, he ended up at the tent of a woman named Jael, whom he asked for water and a place to rest. What follows is one of the most gruesome scenes in the Bible. Jael, knowing he was the fugitive enemy warrior, invited him to lie in a bed, and she covered him with a rug to make him comfortable. When he fell asleep, she executed him. Judges 4:21 says:

> But Jael, Heber's wife, took a tent peg and seized a hammer in her hand, and went secretly to him and drove the peg into his temple, and it went through into the ground; for he was sound asleep and exhausted. So he died.

This is not the kind of story typically used to teach Christian woman how to behave! We want women to be demure, passive and sweet. But is that really what Christian femininity is about? Might not God want women to develop fierceness as well?

Jael reminds us that God has always intended to use His daughters as spiritual warriors—and that in some cases they will deliver the final blow. In this case, Jael acted as God's secret weapon. The enemy had absolutely no suspicion that she was dangerous. He was blindsided. He assumed Jael was weak and fearful. But her courage, surely inspired by the Holy Spirit, aroused in her the passion of a lioness—and she sprang into action.

More Women Warriors

This is not the only time in Scripture when a woman delivers a lethal head injury to the enemy. In fact, this can actually be viewed as a theme. It appears in several places.

First, after Adam and Eve fell into sin, God prophesied to the devil in the Garden of Eden that the seed of the woman would one day crush his head (see Genesis 3:15). The Lord said: "I will put enmity between you and the woman, and between your seed and her seed." This explains why women suffer so much in a fallen world: The enemy has always targeted women because he knows of their potential to wage war against him.

We know the seed of woman did in fact crush the devil when Jesus, the son of the virgin Mary, died on the cross and took the keys of hell and death. But beyond this, women have the opportunity—if they arise in supernatural courage—to inflict more blows on the enemy's head.

Second, in Judges 9 a "certain woman" threw a millstone from the wall and crushed the head of Abimelech, a warrior who was terrorizing God's people. Judges 9:53–54 says:

> But a certain woman threw an upper millstone on Abimelech's head, crushing his skull. Then he called quickly to the young man, his armor bearer, and said to him, "Draw your sword and kill me, so that it will not be said of me, 'A woman slew him.'" So the young man pierced him through, and he died.

We do not know this woman's name. It is doubtful that she was a prominent or wealthy woman—she was just available. When she looked over the wall and saw Abimelech climbing up, she did not wring her hands and wait for a man to come and stop him. She realized that he was within her crosshairs, grabbed a millstone (which was, in primitive terms, a domestic appliance used in the kitchen to grind grain) and hurled it at her enemy in much the same way that David used his slingshot and a smooth stone to fell Goliath. The same spirit of might that empowered David was on display in the case of this brave woman warrior.

The fact that Abimelech was so shocked by her brave deed, and so shamed that he had been outwitted by a woman, gives us some insight into how Satan feels every time a woman breaks free from timidity and decides to attempt something great for God. The devil is actually afraid of what will happen when Christian women discover their true identity in Christ.

Third, in 2 Samuel 20 we read that David's armies were pursuing a rebel named Sheba who had stirred up a revolt in the kingdom. When Sheba entered a certain city named Abel Beth-maacha to organize an attack, David's armies pursued him there and were about to assault the town to capture him. But the Bible says a "wise woman" (2 Samuel 20:16) approached David's general, Joab, and pleaded with him not to destroy the city in order to subdue Sheba.

The unnamed woman told Joab: "I am of those who are peaceable and faithful in Israel. You are seeking to destroy a city, even a mother in Israel. Why would you swallow up the inheritance of the LORD?" (verse 19). When Joab explained that all he wanted was to capture Sheba, the woman promised to subdue him. She told Joab: "Behold, his head will be thrown to you over the wall" (verse 21). Note her determined courage!

Within a short time, another enemy was dealt a lethal head injury by a fierce woman warrior. Sheba's head was tossed over the ramparts of Abel and the violence ended.

If we had but one biblical story of a woman striking the most strategic blow in battle we might not pay much attention to it. But considering these three women along with Jael, we have four separate instances, and we must add a fifth when we consider that Esther's bravery sent Haman to hang on his own gallows. These examples are in Scripture to underscore the obvious: Women were created by God to be dangerous to the devil. Women can engage in spiritual warfare, and they are lethal.

Women Are Dangerous Warriors!

I have met many brave women warriors in my travels around the world, but Natalia Schedrivaya reminds me most of the biblical Deborah. If she had been raised in the United States, chances are she would have been told that women cannot stand behind a pulpit, lead church services or teach men the Bible. Fortunately she never heard those rules. The forty-something preacher never even heard about Jesus until she was in college. Raised in an atheist's home (her father was a Soviet general), Schedrivaya attended Communist schools. She was taught that the Bible is a collection of myths.

But after her conversion, she became a student of the Bible and hopped on a fast track to leadership. In 1997, she became the first woman in Russia to be elected bishop. She went on to lead the Calvary Fellowship of Churches of Russia, a growing network of charismatic congregations that formed after the collapse of Communism in 1989.

Schedrivaya is a different kind of leader. To her, leadership is not about ordering people around like Josef Stalin or Leonid Brezhnev. She says Russians have had enough of dictatorship—and that style of government, she adds, is not what Russian churches need today. "The body of Christ needs to set a new standard of leadership as a position not of control and power, but one of true biblical servanthood," she told me.[1]

I have listened to Schedrivaya preach, and I have held conferences with her in the Ukraine and the United States. What inspires me most is her passionate zeal to win nations to Christ. She told 2,500 people at a Women of Destiny Conference in Kiev: "We often pray to Jesus, 'Lord, please reach the people who have not heard the Gospel.' Why do we pray that? Jesus told us to go! Yet we ask Him to go. Jesus is sitting in heaven. He is waiting for us to go!"

Schedrivaya lives what she preaches. Because she has never married, she considers it easier for her to "go." She is always on the move. She formed her own evangelistic organization called Village Harvest Crusades, through which she plants churches in remote areas of Siberia where there are at least 36,000 towns that do not have a Gospel witness. In many Siberian villages the people worship wind, fire or deer, and they practice an indigenous form of witchcraft. When Schedrivaya preaches the Gospel there, God often confirms her words with miracles of healing.

But this brave lady is not a one-woman show. She has trained dozens of full-time church planters to help fulfill her vision of reaching every village in the vast Siberian tundra—a swath of the globe that spans eight time zones. So far, 70 percent of the people planting churches with her are women.

Schedrivaya's work in this cold region is often dangerous. Once when she ventured into a village to preach, the local Orthodox priest stirred up the people against her and her team, warning them not to believe a "foreign faith." She was almost stoned by the angry mob until a Russian government official intervened, stating that Schedrivaya's team had the right to assemble. Before long, the very individuals who had torn up the team members' Bibles and gathered stones to throw at them were praying the sinner's prayer.

How tragic it is that we have not challenged Christian women in the United States to be this bold! Because of our religious traditions and deeply ingrained chauvinism, we expect women to be passive and quiet when God has called all believers, male and female, to be fearless. Although I do not want Schedrivaya to leave her primary mission field, I have urged her to visit the United States as often as possible. I hope she can help American churches realize the full potential of our women.

Praise: The Secret to a Fighting Spirit

How can you learn to become a spiritual warrior? You may not be called to plant churches in the frozen tundra of Siberia like Natalia Schedrivaya, but you must develop a fierce spirit if you are going to plunder the enemies around you. Bold confidence must flow out of your prayer life. If you are to become one of God's women warriors you must learn to fight depression, anxiety and fear, and the chief way to do this is by praising God. Praise is the training ground for all spiritual warriors.

When Sisera was nailed to the ground after the battle on Mount Tabor, Deborah and Barak burst into a song of praise that is recorded in Judges 5. Scholars say this is one of the oldest poems in the Bible, and they attribute most of it to Deborah herself. She exalted the power of the true God for executing judgment on His enemies, she honored God's people who volunteered to fight so bravely, and she ended the song with a tribute to Jael for her shrewd blow to Sisera.

Deborah was a praiser, and this must have been one of the secrets of her anointing. She knew God, and she spent time with Him. She knew that when she recounted His deeds and magnified His name, He was enthroned in her praises. This became the source of her supernatural courage to fight. The same is true for you. You do not have to muster up your own courage. It will flow through you as you learn to rejoice in God and exalt His name.

This was certainly David's secret, and we have the book of Psalms as evidence. It was this warrior's daily playlist. Whenever he faced difficulties and struggles, or whenever the enemy was winning, David tapped in to the source of courage by singing, shouting and declaring the greatness of God.

The apostle Paul, the greatest spiritual warrior of the New Testament, also understood this principle of praise. His letter to the Philippians is one of the Bible's most unique books. Some scholars call it "the epistle of joy" because the words *joy* and *rejoice* appear in it sixteen times—amazing when you realize that this letter about Christian joy was written from a prison cell!

While Paul was under the watchful eye of Roman guards, bound in chains, he wrote in this letter some of the most uplifting spiritual words ever penned. In four short chapters the author continually exhorts us to praise God no matter how dark our circumstances are. He writes: "I rejoice" (Philippians 1:18); "I rejoice and share my joy with you all" (2:17); "I urge you, rejoice in the same way" (2:18); "Finally, my brethren, rejoice in the Lord" (3:1); and "Rejoice in the Lord always; again I will say, rejoice!" (4:4).

Like a broken record, Paul hammered the same theme over and over and over. Rejoice! The word *rejoice* actually means "to re-joy." It is like a reset button on a computer. When any type of electronic equipment goes out of whack, a reset button will get it back in operation. That is what happens when we rejoice: The joy we have lost is restored and our faith rises again.

Do you feel bound by your circumstances? You must take up the weapon of praise and learn to become a fighter. Remember these points about praise:

1. *Praise shatters despair.* Even though Deborah faced enormous odds in the battle with Sisera's forces, she sang in Judges 5:3: "Hear, O kings; give ear, O rulers! I—to the LORD, I will sing, I will sing praise to the LORD, the God of Israel."

   Know that God is working behind the scenes. The clouds over your head may be dark, but praise will lift you above them so you can see the sun again. When Paul was under house arrest, and could not leave his cell to preach the Gospel, he wrote: "Yes, and I will rejoice, for I know that [my imprisonment] will turn out for my deliverance through your prayers and the provision of the Spirit of Jesus Christ" (Philippians 1:18–19).

2. *Praise shatters doubt.* Deborah was fiercely determined. She trusted the Lord even when some of the tribes of Israel

refused to fight in her army. She stirred herself up spiritually when she declared: "Awake, awake, Deborah; awake, awake, sing a song!" (Judges 5:12).

When you stop praising, you get stuck in the mire of your own problems. All you can see is the here and now. But something supernatural happens when you rejoice in the Lord. You are lifted out of the prison of impossibility and translated into a realm where you "can do all things through Him who strengthens me" (Philippians 4:13).

3. *Praise shatters anxiety.* Joy will calm your anxious heart and allow you to receive the promises of God. When Deborah and Barak finished the battle, and they saw how God had defeated Sisera's army, they sang together: "Thus let all Your enemies perish, O LORD; but let those who love Him be like the rising of the sun in its might" (Judges 5:31).

In 1970 a military chaplain named Merlin Carothers wrote a small book called *Prison to Praise.* Today it has sold more than seventeen million copies in 53 languages. It challenges readers to thank and praise God in the midst of difficulties—and it is full of testimonies of everyday people who experienced miraculous breakthroughs when they obeyed this simple principle.

What Carothers wrote forty years ago is still relevant today:

> The very act of praise releases the power of God into a set of circumstances and enables God to change them. Miracles, power and victory will all be a part of what God does in our lives when we learn to rejoice in all things.

You will derive your courage to fight from this secret weapon of praise.

1. Why do we rarely hear sermons about Deborah?
2. There are several places in the Old Testament where women actually dealt the death blow to the enemy. Why is this significant for you as a woman today?
3. Genesis 3:15 says God placed enmity between the woman and Satan. Have you experienced spiritual warfare? In what ways have you felt that the devil was opposing you?
4. Courageous women must become strong spiritually. Why is the power of praise so important in developing your strength?

A MESSAGE FROM YOUR HEAVENLY FATHER

My precious daughter,

I have called you to be My fierce warrior. Though the enemy rages all around you, there is no reason to fear. I have certain battles reserved for you, and I will give you the strength to strike the enemy. Do not be intimidated by Satan's threats. Just as Deborah arose as a mother in Israel, so you can receive supernatural courage to go forward. As you sing and worship Me, I will inhabit your praises. As you call on My name, I will be your strong tower. As you meditate on My Word, I will place spiritual weapons in your hands, both left and right. I will conquer your depression, fear, worry and inferiority. I will arm you for war, and empower you to fight. Do not shrink back. Do not say, "Because I am a woman, I am weak." Let the weak say, "I am strong." I will give you the courage to deal a lethal blow to the enemy's head.

9

Jehosheba, Daughter of King Joram

The Courage to Protect

There are many phases to a missionary's life. The least of these is to preach, so you don't have to look for those who are especially gifted or learned to become missionaries. Kindness is the big thing.

—Malla Moe (1863–1953), missionary to Swaziland and other parts of Africa

*L*inda Graham believes in miracles, but her faith was stretched beyond her wildest imagination when she arrived in Haiti with three other women from Durham, North Carolina, in January 2010. They were on a routine mission to deliver clothing and medical supplies to an orphanage. They had no idea they were walking into one of the worst natural disasters in modern history.

Their plane touched down in Port-au-Prince on January 12 at 4:00 P.M.—fifteen minutes ahead of schedule. A Haitian pastor met them at the airport, loaded their bags into his vehicle and prepared to drive them to the town of Carrefour when everything began to shake. At first Linda thought people were pushing the car until she noticed the trees were shaking, too.

A 7.0 earthquake had just hit the city. Linda and her friends had no access to news broadcasts. All they could see were buildings collapsing and people running into the streets. Many people were covered with blood and white dust. One woman stood naked in the street with a stunned expression. Linda and her friends gave her some clothes.

Unable to drive to the orphanage, the pastor took the women to a church where about two thousand people were singing and praying; the crude shelter had survived the quake. Later that evening the women relocated to a soccer field where people were sleeping on sheets under the stars. Injured people were everywhere, but still the sound of praises filled the air.

The next morning wounded people lined up in front of the four white women, assuming they were nurses. Linda, feeling completely inadequate in the face of such need, reached for their luggage and the supplies they had brought: bandages, antibacterial medicine, alcohol preps and $500 worth of underwear.

Amazingly, they also had packed 25 pounds of rubber gloves. The women sprang into action. They began praying for people and applying bandages and Neosporin.

"I am convinced there was a loaves-and-fishes kind of miracle going on," Linda told me after she was airlifted to Florida several days later. "All our supplies were multiplied. We even used Band-Aids on an amputated leg."

The biggest test of the women's faith came later that morning when two Haitian women went into labor. Linda was asked to deliver the babies—in an abandoned hospital. There were at least three hundred dead bodies piled near the building's entrance, but Linda was determined to see life triumph over the misery she saw all around her.

"It was an awful place," she said of the badly damaged Ministry of Health Hospital. "The three rusted tables in the maternity room were covered in bodily fluids. There was no electricity or running water in there. All I had was a pair of scissors and some fabric."

Linda swallowed hard, prayed in the Holy Spirit and called on the Lord for help and protection for these mothers and their children. She prayed harder when she realized that the first baby was in a breech position. "I just made a declaration," she told me. "I prayed, 'You will move into the right position and you will be born in Jesus' name!'" A healthy girl was born in a few minutes.

The second pregnant woman then needed attention, and her Christian husband translated Linda's English instructions to his wife. To help the mother breathe properly, Linda told her to say "Hallelujah." When a baby boy was born, the overjoyed father asked Linda to name the child. It was a prophetic moment that helped Linda gain insight into what God is doing today in this ravaged nation.

"I told him to name the boy Judah—which means 'praise,'" Linda said. "I told him, 'We have to praise our way through this.'"

When Linda shared her story with me I realized God was working a million miracles in Haiti that we never heard about on CNN when news of the disaster dominated the airwaves for the rest of that month. A boy named Judah was just one of those miracles. And he came into the world because one brave woman was willing to take decisive action.

Sometimes Love Is Fierce

Thrown into the horror of Haiti's disaster, Linda Graham did not have to work up the courage to care for sick people or to deliver babies on the spot. She did not even have time to think about her reaction. She just jumped in and offered the care that was required. It came naturally for her because she is a woman, and because she is full of the Holy Spirit. That can be an explosive combination. Women who know God intimately have the potential to do many things they would not normally think they can do.

This was the case for Jehosheba, a righteous woman who is mentioned in the Bible in just a few short verses. She lived in a dark time when Israel was backslidden and headed for God's judgment. But when she found herself between a rock and a hard place, she did not cower in fear or run for the hills. She experienced a supernatural power surge, and her courageous actions literally saved a nation. Second Kings 11:1–3 says:

> When Athaliah the mother of Ahaziah saw that her son was dead, she rose and destroyed all the royal offspring. But Jehosheba, the daughter of King Joram, sister of Ahaziah, took Joash the son of Ahaziah and stole him from among the king's sons who were being put to death, and placed him and his nurse in the bedroom. So they hid him from Athaliah, and he was not put to death. So he was hidden with her in the house of the LORD six years, while Athaliah was reigning over the land.

It is hard to imagine that a queen would slaughter her own grandchildren, but that is exactly what the wicked Athaliah did because of her insatiable lust for control over the kingdom. She was the daughter of Jezebel, whose hatred of God's prophets intimidated even Elijah. Athaliah was a pawn of the pagan god Baal. The power operating in her was not a mere human phenomenon—it was a demonic fury bent on wiping out the seed of King David. But as the dark storm clouds gathered, Jehosheba sprang into action.

Notice the Bible does not say that Jehosheba made an appointment with the elders for advice. She did not sit on her hands for a couple of days, wondering if a woman should attempt such a daring rescue. This was no time for dawdling. A baby's life was at stake, and the lineage of the Messiah was in danger. God needed someone with courage to take action. And He needed her to act fast.

In the years that followed, God helped Jehosheba with her mission. The fact that she was able to hide the infant from Athaliah for six years—right under her nose in the Temple—is proof that God was supernaturally shielding him. But Athaliah's wicked plot was outwitted because of a woman's bravery in the face of terror.

The story does not end well for Athaliah. When the boy Joash turned seven, Jehosheba's husband, Jehoida, who served as the Lord's priest, staged a dramatic coup. Athaliah was executed, the idols of Baal were torn down, and the boy king was crowned and installed in power (see 2 Kings 11:9–21). Israel's royal family was saved and the seed that eventually led to Christ was preserved. And all this happened as God empowered a woman to intervene.

Why is this story in the Bible? It is evidence of God's specific call on women to be fierce protectors. We mentioned earlier a similar story in the book of Exodus, set around the time Moses was born. Pharaoh had ordered the slaughter of all Jewish boys at birth. He commanded the Jewish midwives to carry out his edict as they were attending to pregnant Hebrew women.

But the brave midwives, Shiphrah and Puah, performed one of the first recorded acts of civil disobedience. Their motherly instincts kicked in, and a fierce protectiveness overpowered any fear they felt. Exodus 1:17–20 says:

> But the midwives feared God, and did not do as the king of Egypt had commanded them, but let the boys live. So the king of Egypt called for the midwives and said to them, "Why have you done this thing, and let the boys live?" The midwives said to Pharaoh, "Because the Hebrew women are not as the Egyptian women; for they

are vigorous and give birth before the midwife can get to them." So God was good to the midwives, and the people multiplied, and became very mighty.

These women could have been killed on the spot for their subversive actions. They deliberately disobeyed the royal edict and then embellished their story. They were sneaky. They found a way around the Pharaoh's wicked plan, and saved lives. They were the ultimate pro-life activists. And from the context of the story, they seemed to be acting on their own. The Bible does not say they were instructed by their husbands or male elders of Israel to carry out their brave deeds. No men are mentioned. These women, acting as God's secret agents, quickly took the initiative and stopped genocide.

Is there room in your worldview for brave women like Jehosheba, Shiphrah and Puah? Through the ages, the ideal of femininity is often expressed in passivity. The Victorian era is a classic example. Women were expected to serve society as domestic decorations. The virtue of womanhood was best exemplified when women sat in their parlors drinking tea, reading poetry and wearing corsets under their taffeta gowns.

This fallacy was updated in the "June Cleaver" era of 1950s America, when the ideal woman was portrayed as the perfectly coiffed stay-at-home mom. Her husband would conquer the world and earn the family's income; she was supposed to find fulfillment in ironing, baking casseroles and raising children—while wearing a starched dress and pearl necklace.

There is nothing wrong with pearls, or with women ironing or cooking. And women who have children should certainly take the responsibility seriously. But the message in both Victorian England and suburban America was that women should not attempt anything brave. They should stay indoors, out of the heat of the sun, and out of trouble. They should let their men solve the world's problems while they attend to details like folding linens and polishing silverware.

Secular Americans do not think that way today, for the most part, but sadly many Christians do. Some congregations not only frown on women holding positions of authority in their churches, as we have seen, but also discourage women from pursuing careers or running for political office. Women who take any initiative are viewed with suspicion. This attitude has squelched the calling and spiritual gifting of countless women who were told that bravery is a masculine quality, and that in order to please God they should always defer to men.

Thank God Jehosheba did not attend that women's prayer group! If she had, the other women would have told her: "Don't meddle in that situation with Athaliah. That's not your job. If God wants to stop her from killing Joash, He will direct Jehoiada or one of the other priests to intervene." And if Shiphrah and Puah had attended some of our modern conservative churches, they would have been advised to stay out of Pharaoh's way. "Women aren't supposed to make trouble," their colleagues might have said.

From my reading of Scripture, I find that God does indeed call His women to stir up trouble. He gave women mouths to challenge evil and hands to deliver the babies that the devil meant to destroy. He gave them brains to plan strategies for the overthrow of demonic powers. And He gave women a unique grace to feel compassion for the vulnerable, the poor and those in danger.

The Power of Motherly Instinct

I have watched several documentaries on the television channel Animal Planet that include footage of mother animals protecting their young. Do you know what happens when another animal bothers a baby lion cub? The lioness springs into action. Her claws come out, her fangs protrude and she lets out a roar that can be heard miles away.

It is true that a male lion's roar is louder than a female's, but the female's fierceness is formidable. She uses her roar not only to call her young, but also to call other members of the pride to come and help her fight. She is not acting "masculine" when she does this. God created female lions with an inborn protective instinct; in fact, female lions provide almost all the protection of young cubs while males hunt for food.

Scientists have discovered that the female brain is wired to protect children, sometimes fiercely. The phenomenon, known as "maternal aggression," has been linked to a certain peptide that is associated with lactation. Stephen Gammie of the University of Wisconsin told *Scientific American* that studies in mice concluded that females were more aggressive in protecting their babies when this peptide is not blocked or hindered by other hormones.[1] (In fact, other studies have shown that women who neglect their children or abuse them often do it during bouts of postpartum depression when hormones have blocked the normal maternal aggression response.[2])

Could it be that God has uniquely formulated a woman's body chemistry to make her fierce? It would seem so. It would also explain why, throughout history, women have hurdled all types of obstacles in order to save the weak, nurse the sick and protect the underdogs of society. When children are in danger, when women are abused, when girls are exploited, when families are being destroyed by drugs or alcohol or when society is in danger, it is often a woman who volunteers first to rescue the most vulnerable.

I doubt that Corrie ten Boom (1892–1983) thought too much about the biochemical reasons for her overwhelming compassion. A devout Christian who grew up in Holland, her first assignment in ministry was to care for disabled children. When the Nazis invaded her country in 1940, they banned her from operating a club for girls; a few months later the SS guards on patrol in the streets of Haarlem required all Jews to wear fabric stars on their sleeves to identify them. Hitler and his dreaded forces were preparing to round up all Jews from Holland and send them to concentration camps.

It was actually Corrie's father, Casper ten Boom, a watchmaker, who first decided that he and his family would protect Jews from the German police by hiding them in their home on the street known as Barteljorisstraat. The Ten Boom family, working within the network of the Haarlem underground, fashioned what was called *de schuilplaats*, "the hiding place," a closet-sized space behind a false wall in Corrie's upstairs room. Because Corrie believed that Jews were God's chosen people, and that they had preserved the Old Testament for the world, she readily agreed to participate in the covert mission. She spent a great deal of time caring for these individuals, even convincing a sympathetic civil servant to give her food ration cards illegally that she could then give to the secret Jewish tenants.

On February 28, 1944, Nazi guards burst into the Ten Boom house and arrested Corrie, her father, her sister Betsie, and three other members of the family. While they were carted off to Scheveningen Prison, two Jewish men, two Jewish women and two members of the Dutch underground were crouched in the hiding place. The Ten Booms paid a dear price for their defiance. Casper died ten days after his arrest; Corrie and Betsie were sent to the lice-infested Ravensbrück Concentration Camp in Germany, where Betsie died. Corrie was released on New Year's Eve, 1944, because of a clerical error. A week later, all the women her age in Ravensbrück were killed.

I have been to Corrie's home in Holland, and I have crawled into the tiny space behind her bedroom wall where many Jews and resistance workers hid quietly during Nazi inspections. I have read Corrie's miraculous story, *The Hiding Place*, and seen the movie about her life. I have marveled at the courage she demonstrated in the face of evil. But I do not know if I can ever fathom how this soft-spoken daughter of a watchmaker decided to defy the Nazi monster in order to save Jewish people.

Corrie said herself that it was the power of God's love that drove her to lay her life on the line, and to sacrifice her own safety to protect others. In *The Hiding Place* she wrote these words that her father spoke to her:

> "Corrie, . . . do you know what hurts so very much? It's love. Love is the strongest force in the world, and when it is blocked that means pain. There are two things we can do when this happens. We can kill the love so that it stops hurting. But then of course part of us dies, too. Or, Corrie, we can ask God to open up another route for that love to travel."[3]

I believe love is the secret of a woman's fierceness. When you allow God's love—however painful—to so perfectly control you, and when you trade your selfish concerns for God's priorities, the compassion you feel for people—especially for those who are in danger or at risk—will drive you to rescue them. You will stop caring so much for your own safety. This compelling love is mentioned in Proverbs 24:11, which says: "Deliver those who are being taken away to death, and those who are staggering to slaughter, oh hold them back."

When someone is being attacked, abused or mistreated, often the human reaction is to look the other way. We do not like conflict. We do not want to get involved in someone else's problems or misfortunes. We do not want to get hurt. But God's transcendent love calls us to take the less comfortable route. Like the Good Samaritan in Jesus' parable, we reach out to the injured traveler, no matter his identity, and heal his wounds.

Christian compassion is what has built most of the hospitals and orphanages in the world. It is the motivating force behind shelters from domestic violence and safe houses for victims of sex trafficking. It is why believers protest racism or the exploitation of child workers. It is the reason Christian families adopt babies from war-torn countries. It is why thousands of men and women volunteer every year to take the Gospel to dangerous countries.

If you read the writings of great Christian women activists—the Quaker women who opposed slavery, the Methodist Holiness women who worked to stop alcoholism in the era of Prohibition, the Presbyterians of the 1800s who started hospitals in Africa, the many female missionaries who established homes to rescue Indian girls from prostitution—or if you listen to the passionate preaching of modern evangelical women who are working tirelessly to stop the global sex trafficking industry, you will find a common thread. All have been consumed by a holy love. It compels them to rescue the weak and the innocent. If you are willing to ask for it, it will consume you as well.

LET'S TALK ABOUT IT

1. Can you think of a time when you experienced "maternal aggression" and protected someone from danger? Share your story.
2. Why is Jehosheba considered so brave? And what was the result of her actions?
3. Why do you think some Christians are uncomfortable when women do courageous things? Is there a particular group of

people—children, the elderly, abused women, the poor—for whom you feel called to take action?

4. Corrie ten Boom risked her life to protect Jews from Nazism because she loved them. How do you think you would have responded if you had been in her situation?

A Message from Your Heavenly Father

My precious daughter,

I wired you to be courageous. Even though you may feel weak, I am strong within you. Remember: Jesus is the Lion of the tribe of Judah. Because He lives in your heart by My Spirit, you are more than a conqueror. Don't limit yourself. The weak can say, "I am strong." I have armed you with faith and courage, and I have placed a protective instinct within you. If you will allow Me to fill you with My love, I will use you to oppose injustice, help the weak, heal the sick and protect those who are being abused and exploited. Expect Me to use you in miraculous ways. Just as Jehosheba saved the royal family with her bravery, and Shiphrah and Puah saved a generation of children with their cunning, I will give you boldness to face every challenge.

10

Mary, the Mother of Jesus

The Courage to Surrender

The greatness of man's power is the measure of his surrender. It isn't a question of who you are, or of what you are, but whether God controls you.

—Henrietta Mears (1890–1963), Christian educator and founder of Gospel Light Publishing Company

Normal births are fascinating, whether they occur in hospitals or homes or the backseats of taxis. But when I consider the birth of Jesus, I am in total awe—not just because of the bumpy ride from Nazareth on a donkey, Mary's lack of a doctor (and no anesthesia!) and the crudeness of the manger, but also because of how Jesus was conceived. Mary was a virgin. Joseph, the "father" in the Christmas narrative, had no part in the conception.

Secularists and liberal theologians have mocked the virgin birth for centuries. Thomas Jefferson called it a fable, while Episcopal heretic John Shelby Spong called it an "entrance myth." The concept of a woman giving birth to a baby without a man's involvement is ludicrous to unbelievers. It contradicts all laws of biology.

Yet Mary did not doubt God's word. She asked the angel how she would bear this child, and he said: "The Holy Spirit will come upon you, and the power of the Most High will overshadow you" (Luke 1:35).

I would have asked for more scientific information, but Mary did not quibble over details. She believed Gabriel's announcement and submitted to God in childlike faith.

The Greek word for *overshadow*, *episkiazo*, is a reference to the cloud of God's presence that materialized in Moses' Tabernacle. The *Amplified Bible* translates Luke 1:35 as: He "will overshadow you [like a shining cloud]." This same cloud hovered over the Ark of the Covenant, led God's people through the wilderness and filled Solomon's Temple with shimmering Shekinah glory.

The same cloud of glory that caused Moses' face to shine hovered over a virgin and deposited a divine seed into her womb. The God who hid behind a veil in the Old Testament clothed Himself in human flesh in the New Testament.

When the Savior was born, there was a normal amount of blood, sweat and tears—because Mary was human. But this birth was surrounded with wonder because Joseph was not the father. He came from a line of Hebrew kings, but his pedigree was not enough to save the human race. He could not contribute to this incarnation miracle.

Doubters assume that Joseph got Mary pregnant out of wedlock, and then concocted the story about an angel to cover his sin. If that were true, Christianity itself would be a lie: If God were not Jesus' biological father, He could not have redeemed us. Jesus— who was born of a woman so that He might identify fully with our sins—had to be both man and God. That is the only way the Lamb of God could pay for the sins of the world.

This is the most glorious revelation of the nativity. Bible teacher R. T. Kendall puts it this way: "The virgin birth of Christ shows that salvation can never come through human effort."[1] God performed this science-defying miracle without our help. All we can do is stand in awe, like the virgin Mary, and receive His amazing love and forgiveness.

Mary, the mother of Jesus, is one of the most misunderstood and wrongly portrayed characters in the Bible. Because she provided a womb for the Savior, many people deify her. Roman Catholic doctrine states that she herself was conceived "immaculately" (meaning that she was conceived free from the stain of original sin), that she remained sinless throughout her life and that she was "assumed" into heaven without dying. Roman Catholic dogma offers the further concept that she serves as "Coredemptrix," a collaborator with Jesus in the redemption of humanity. None of these ideas is supported by Scripture.

If you visit a Roman Catholic church in Latin America, you will likely see Mary seated on a heavenly throne, staring down on the corpse of a dead Jesus. Because of early Christian heresies and medieval superstitions, Mary came to be viewed as a goddess figure, as if her divine pregnancy put her on a level above all other human beings.

This is ironic when you consider that this teenager named Mary was chosen to be the mother of Jesus simply because she was available—and because she was willing to surrender her life to the will of God no matter the cost to her family or reputation. She was a humble girl who called herself a "bondslave of the Lord" and said to Him, in total selflessness, "May it be done to me according to Your word" (Luke 1:38).

Mary was not power-hungry, ambitious or seeking a place of fame or fortune. She was poor in spirit. She had an innocent willingness to please God. When the angel announced the divine plan in generalities, she did not ask, "What's in this for me?" She did not put up a fight, roll her eyes or try to bargain with the angel. She was not looking for book deals or ways to sell movie rights to her story. Her heart was pure. She had died to her own desires.

Mary's abandonment to God's plan is even more obvious when compared to the attitude of Zacharias, the priest who was chosen to be the father of John the Baptist. When the angel appeared to him in the Temple, the Bible says he was gripped with fear and he questioned the fact that his wife, Elizabeth, would have a baby since she was past childbearing years (see Luke 1:12, 18). Zacharias was struck dumb for at least nine months because of his doubts; meanwhile, Mary openly embraced the promise God sent through the angel Gabriel—and instead of losing her voice, she uttered the Magnificat, one of the most beautiful psalms in the Bible. It is recorded in Luke 1:46–49:

> "My soul exalts the Lord, and my spirit has rejoiced in God my Savior. For He has had regard for the humble state of His bondslave; for behold, from this time on all generations will count me blessed. For the Mighty One has done great things for me; and holy is His name."

Mary is, to all Christians, the quintessential role model of consecration. But this does not mean she was sinless or immaculate. The gospels tell us that Mary and some of Jesus' other family members tried to talk Him out of fulfilling His ministry when He began itinerating, and that Jesus subtly rebuked them when they came to His door. (Mark 3:21 says Jesus' family had come to take custody of Him because they felt He had "lost His senses.") Mary did not always fully understand Jesus' mission, and she must have been conflicted about some aspects of His message.

But her doubts were obviously resolved after the death of Jesus. This humble woman who had surrendered her body to carry the Messiah actually stood at the foot of the cross when He was crucified. Most of Jesus' male followers were not there. The gospels tell us that the disciple John came to the cross, along with the virgin Mary, Mary, the wife of Cleopas, and Mary Magdalene. Everyone else had fled. Only the fully consecrated are willing to identify that closely with death.

Imagine! After thousands of people had crowded around Jesus to hear His sermons or to eat His free lunches or to experience supernatural healings, there were no crowds gathered on the hill called Golgotha that day. There were only a handful of brave disciples who had already died to their own reputations and fears. And the virgin Mary was among them.

She not only started her journey with God in consecration, but carried out that consecrated life to the end. She embraced the fullness of her son's message by being willing to deny herself, carry the cross and follow Him no matter where His path led. In the truest sense Mary is the model disciple, and this is underscored by the fact that she is among the 120 followers of Christ who prayed for the outpouring of Pentecost in the Upper Room (see Acts 1:14). Not only did Mary start out well, but she followed through and went the distance.

This is the hallmark of a surrendered life. And it is a requirement for all women who want their lives to count for God. A surrendered heart is not an option for a true disciple. We must be willing to wave a white flag over our lives and let go. We must come to the place where we can say with Mary, "May it be done to me according to Your word."

Consecration Is Not a Dirty Word

As we have noted, God did not give the virgin Mary much information when He presented His complex plan to her. And yet she did not protest. Her will was like putty in God's hands.

The angel could have said: "Here's the deal, Mary. The Holy Spirit is going to cause you to get pregnant out of wedlock. Your family and your village will think you are immoral. Your fiancé is going to want to divorce you. You will have to travel on a donkey for a number of days in your ninth month. When the baby is born, Herod is going to try to kill Him so you will have to live as a refugee in Egypt. When He starts His ministry, most people in Nazareth are going to be angry with Him. He will be hated by the Jewish establishment, and they are going to execute Him. You will be there to watch Him die."

God did not present those facts to Mary. He gave her very few details. But her attitude was amazingly submissive. She basically said: "Okay, Lord, whatever You say." Is this your attitude when you approach God?

Christians used to talk a lot about surrender. They called it the consecrated life, and they sang about it in hymns such as "I Surrender All," "Have Thine Own Way, Lord" or "Wherever He Leads, I'll Go." These songs fueled the missionary movements of the past. Today? Not so much.

In many American churches, "altars" are a strange concept. They are referred to as "stages," and they are used for fog machines or music performances. Altar calls no longer fit in the time constraints of our trendy eighty-minute services. Meanwhile, talk of surrender has been replaced by messages about self-empowerment and self-motivation.

The Good Life has replaced The God Life. The Path to Prosperity has become more popular than The Calvary Road. We are more interested in getting a breakthrough than brokenness.

Yet God is calling us back to consecration. Genuine worship, according to Romans 12:1, involves a wholehearted abandonment of self. Paul wrote: "Therefore I urge you, brethren, by the mercies of God, to present your bodies a living and holy sacrifice, acceptable to God, which is your spiritual service of worship."

When priests were set apart for God's service in the Old Covenant, they were consecrated in a solemn ceremony. The word for *consecration* in Exodus 28:41 means "to fill the hand." The word is a picture of an empty hand receiving God's blessings and then giving them back to the Lord in unconditional surrender.

Here is my question to you: Are your hands open and raised to God, like Mary's? Or are you making a fist? Have you given back to the Lord what He has given you? Or are your hands tightly clenched? It might be a good idea to examine how you are holding every aspect of your life:

- *Your time.* Does God have your life 24/7? Does He have your weekends? Have you made room in your life to spend time with Him? Or has prayer been crowded out by your favorite television shows, time with friends or the demands of work?

- *Your talents.* Are you using your natural and spiritual gifts to reach others for Christ? Or do you hide your talents, like the unwise steward in Jesus' parable? Have you assumed that, because others seemed more gifted, you should be a spectator while they serve?

- *Your money.* The only way to know if you are truly surrendered to God's will is if your wallet is open. Lack of generosity toward God's work reveals a much deeper problem.

- *Your future.* Are you driving your career plans—or have you allowed God to take the steering wheel? Ambition can take you a long way, but it must be yielded to His will or it will lead to tragedy. You must agree with what Jesus prayed at Gethsemane: "Not My will, but Yours be done" (Luke 22:42).

- *Your relationships.* Do you allow friends or romantic relationships to lead you away from purity, integrity and spiritual faithfulness? The Bible says that friendship with the world is hostility toward God (see James 4:4). As painful as it may be, true surrender will involve cutting some ties.

- *Your sexuality.* Many Christians believe that they can be faithful followers of God while practicing immorality. But living the consecrated life means repenting of all known sin daily—and fleeing from fornication, adultery, pornography and all forms of lust.

- *Your children.* While we have been commanded to raise our kids for God, we also must entrust them to His care. After all, they are really His children, not ours. Once you have done your part, give them back to Him. I have had to consciously put my girls on the altar whenever I have doubted that God will take care of them. It is one thing to give your own life to Christ. It is another thing to surrender those you love to His will and purpose. It requires a whole new level of trust. But it is the path that Abraham, the father of our faith, was required to walk when he put his son Isaac on the altar.

True faith always involves gut-wrenching surrender. I urge you to take the right posture: Get your hands open, lift them up to heaven and say with all your heart: "Lord, I'm all Yours."

Here I Am, Lord. Send Me!

More than a dozen years ago I found myself at a church altar in Orlando, Florida. God had been dealing with me about leaving my comfort zone. I had a great job with nice benefits, yet I felt spiritually unfulfilled. I knew there was an amazing adventure in front of me, but I had placed serious limitations on my obedience.

As I buried my face in the carpet in that church, I realized God was requiring unconditional surrender. He wanted me to wave a white flag. I knew what I had to say, but it was difficult to form the words. Finally, I coughed them up. I said the same thing the prophet Isaiah prayed long ago: *Here I am, send me!* (see Isaiah 6:8).

This is a dangerous prayer. It is risky because God immediately takes you up on it. I believe that when you utter these simple words, heaven takes a Polaroid picture of you with your hands up—and an amazing process begins. He closes in on you in order to crush your fears and demolish your selfishness.

When I prayed this prayer in 1998, I immediately had a vision while I was still on the floor. I saw a sea of African faces. I knew I would be going to Africa, and I was scared to death. I had no idea how I would get there, what I would say or who would pay for the trip. So I swallowed hard and prayed again: *Here I am, send me!*

Less than two years later I found myself standing on a huge stage in a sports arena in Port Harcourt, Nigeria, speaking to seven thousand pastors. I did not enjoy the bumpy flight, and my knees were knocking when I preached. I felt as if I had been pushed way out on a limb. But even though I was terrified, my fear was mixed with incredible joy. The Lord had overcome my resistance, and He was using me! Since that trip I have ministered in more than 25 countries.

Grace is so amazing. Not only does God give us the power to serve Him, He also plants in us the desire to surrender to His will even if we are scared of the consequences. This is what the apostle Paul described when he said: "It is God who is at work in you, both to will and to work for His good pleasure" (Philippians 2:13).

God has an uncanny way of wooing us into submission. Our flesh may protest; our fears may paralyze us. But in the end, if we will simply lift our hands in surrender, grace will take over. He will give us power, strength and a willing heart. And the results are supernatural because it is God at work in us.

The Church has advanced throughout history because of people who surrendered to God. One of them was the brave David Brainerd (1718–1747), a missionary to American Indians during the First Great Awakening. Although he died of tuberculosis at age 29, his legacy of total consecration lives on in his journal, which was published by his friend Jonathan Edwards.

Brainerd recorded this very dangerous prayer in his diary:

> Here am I, send me; send me to the ends of the earth; send me to the rough, the savage pagans of the wilderness; send me from all that is called comfort on earth; send me even to death itself, if it be but in Thy service, and to promote Thy kingdom.[2]

We rarely hear prayers like that today. Brainerd's passion would be considered politically incorrect fanaticism. We do not promote self-sacrifice; we have a new gospel of self-fulfillment. But God is calling us to reclaim the attitude Mary modeled for us all. What if you raised your hands and left all your fears, worries, excuses, stipulations, limitations and conditions on heaven's altar—and invited God to use your life in any way He wanted?

I dare you to try it.

LET'S TALK ABOUT IT

1. Depending on your church background, you may have developed some erroneous notions about the virgin Mary. Talk about these.

2. Why do you think Mary can be viewed as a model disciple? What was it about her attitude that makes her an example for all of us?

3. How would you define *consecration*, and why is it so important in the Christian life?

4. After reading this chapter, are there areas of your life that you feel you need to surrender to God? Share these with your group, and have a time of prayer in which you give these things to Him.

A MESSAGE FROM YOUR HEAVENLY FATHER

My precious daughter,

My hand is on your life, and I want to use you. I have formed and shaped you for a special purpose. I am the potter, and you are the clay. You will never fully understand your purpose apart from Me. But when you spend time in My presence, and when you allow Me to possess every part of you, I will reveal My will to you. And I will empower you to be My instrument. I am not asking you to jump through hoops. I am simply asking you to be available. I want you to respond as Mary did when she said, "Let it be done to me according to Your word." Surrender your fears. Leave your anxieties and worries at My altar. Give Me your life without reservation, and let Me shape it into what I desire. I know what is best for you. And you can trust Me to make you the woman you were designed to be.

⟨⟨ 11 ⟩⟩

Mary of Bethany

The Courage to Worship

> God doesn't want what you are going to be or
> what you would like to be. . . . He wants all that
> you are today.
>
> —Australian worship leader Darlene Zschech

always find it amusing that many tradition-bound Christians
do not believe that a woman can lead worship. One Russian-
American woman I know told me that when she came forward to
lead the music in a particular church, the pastor told her she could
not say anything between the songs. ("We will let you sing, but
women cannot speak from the platform," he told her.) Another
friend of mine who is a professional musician was literally whisked
off the stage of a church in New York City during a wedding re-
hearsal because, in the words of the church deacons, "Women are
not allowed to sing from the pulpit."

This is an odd concept when you consider that one of the first worship leaders mentioned in the Bible is Moses' sister, Miriam, who praised God with her tambourine after Pharaoh's army was drowned in the Red Sea. And, as we have noted, both Deborah and Hannah have songs recorded in Scripture (see Judges 5; 1 Samuel 2:1–10). God does not restrict women from worshiping Him. In fact, He seems to encourage it!

Even more ironic is the fact that churches that do not allow women to lead worship will sing choruses written by women. One of the most prolific hymn writers of all time, Fanny Crosby (1820–1915), has been called "the mother of congregational singing in America." She penned her first hymn in 1844,[1] and wrote more than nine thousand hymns during her lifetime. Because some people objected to the fact that she was a woman writer and musician, she used at least two hundred pseudonyms during her career.[2] (This was also because some people objected to seeing her name so often in hymnals.)

Crosby, who became associated with the largely Methodist-influenced Holiness movement, was also a public speaker and evangelist. She devoted the latter years of her life to working with alcoholics, prostitutes and criminals in various evangelical outreaches in New York City, including the Bowery Mission and the Water Street Mission, as well as in prisons. But she is best known for the songs she wrote, including "Pass Me Not," "Near the Cross," "Rescue the Perishing," "Jesus Is Calling" and "Blessed Assurance."

Not surprisingly, Crosby had her critics. Religious music in her day was dominated by tough Calvinists who disliked the emotionalism displayed in Holiness churches.[3] They turned up their noses at those who emphasized personal Christian experience over rigid doctrine. In fact, some have even accused Crosby of single-handedly "emasculating" worship in the American church by introducing what they felt was a softer, feminine style. One smug reviewer said her songs were "gushy" and "crudely sentimental."[4] Crosby was not fazed by criticism because she knew the Holy Spirit used her lyrics to lead thousands of people to salvation.

I will let the theologians continue the ivory tower arguments about sexism and hymnology. Meanwhile, it should be obvious to the most casual reader of the Bible that God has called both men and women to worship Him, and that Jesus Christ specifically called attention to women's worship. It was special to Him.

This was demonstrated clearly when a woman who was a "sinner," generally assumed to be a prostitute, came to Jesus while He was dining with Simon the Pharisee. This troubled woman heard that Jesus was visiting in the area, so she barged into Simon's house uninvited, opened her bottle of perfume, poured it on Jesus and began wiping His feet with her hair as she moistened them with her tears (see Luke 7:36–39).

This unidentified woman knew who Jesus really was; His arrogant religious host did not. Her actions were scandalous because she had a dirty past, and yet she felt the liberty to approach Jesus and touch Him. She understood that Jesus was merciful, and that He had forgiven her. She knew He was the Savior of the world. And that knowledge led to an extravagant, expensive, audacious display of heartfelt gratitude and tender emotion. Whenever we see Jesus for who He really is, the natural response is always raw, uninhibited worship.

But Simon did not have any room in his stuffy theology for this woman's outlandish behavior. Like Fanny Crosby's hymns, this sinner's emotional display was, in his view, gushy and sentimental. Jewish rabbis in the time of Jesus looked down on women and criticized them for being flighty, uneducated and overly emotional. But Jesus did not view women that way. He not only received this woman's worship, but He also used it as an example to show how sinners should respond to God when they are forgiven. Jesus praised the woman and rebuked Simon. By doing so He also made it clear that He does not reject the worship of women or view it disdainfully.

The unnamed woman was literally gushing with worship for her Savior. She knew she did not deserve forgiveness. She was truly thankful, and this uncorked a flood of adoration and tears. This should remind us that the best worship is never restrained or subdued. God does not want cold hearts and mechanical praise. He invites us to gush.

Worship Flows from Brokenness

Extravagant worshipers almost always minister to God out of their own personal struggles. This was certainly the case with Fanny Crosby. When she was just six weeks old she caught a cold virus and contracted serious inflammation in her eyes. A doctor applied a mustard poultice to treat her, and the substance damaged her optic nerves. She went blind and never recovered her sight. This is why she is always pictured in dark glasses.[5]

Amazingly, Fanny's disability did not put a damper on her joy or stop the music in her heart. When she was only eight years old she wrote a poem that said, in part: "Oh what a happy soul I am, although I cannot see; I am resolved that in this world contented I will be."[6] Later, she told her friends that she was actually grateful for her blindness because she believed God used it to prepare her for a unique ministry:

> It seemed intended by the blessed providence of God that I should be blind all my life, and I thank Him for the dispensation. If perfect earthly sight were offered me tomorrow I would not accept it. I might not have sung hymns to the praise of God if I had been distracted by the beautiful and interesting things about me.[7]

Most people never reach this place of spiritual maturity. We whine and complain when things fail to go our way. We focus on our needs, our problems, our schedules, our paychecks, our bills and our selfish goals. We worship the creature (ourselves) and not the Creator. Yet we know that the Father is seeking people who will worship Him in spirit and in truth. (Jesus made that profound statement *to a woman* in John 4:23–24!) He wants us to lose ourselves. He calls us to shift our focus away from self—with all its dysfunction—and behold Him. Because we were created to give Him glory, we will never truly understand our purpose in life until we learn to worship.

So how do we make this shift? How do we learn to worship? Ironically, the gospels answer that question by pointing us to one of Christ's most devoted women followers, Mary of Bethany. She is, like no one else in the gospel narratives, the quintessential worshiper.

The first time we are introduced to her, she is home with her brother, Lazarus, and her sister, Martha. Jesus had obviously gone there with some of His disciples, and He was teaching them. If Jesus had been any other rabbi, this Bible study would have been a male-only affair. Jewish teachers in that time period did not have female disciples, and they did not allow women to receive instruction from the Torah.

But Jesus was not like any other Jewish rabbi. When we first meet Mary, she is "seated at the Lord's feet, listening to His word" (Luke 10:39) inside the house. Martha is upset about this unusual behavior; she cannot fathom the concept of a woman taking the posture of a disciple—certainly not when there is work to be done. But Jesus did not rebuke Mary or tell her to go back into the kitchen where most women of that time period felt most comfortable. He affirmed Mary's decision to step outside normal cultural roles.

He said to Martha in Luke 10:41–42: "Martha, Martha, you are worried and bothered about so many things; but only one thing is necessary, for Mary has chosen the good part, which shall not be taken away from her."

Jesus broke centuries of tradition when He uttered those words. Women had always been relegated to the back of the house and the rear of the synagogue. They were not included in the religious life of Israel, and chauvinistic rabbis wanted to push them farther to the side, behind a partition or on a second-floor balcony. Jesus contradicted this idea. Mary could sense that Jesus wanted her near Him; she felt the magnetic pull of His welcoming presence. She walked bravely into the room where Jesus' disciples had gathered (and most likely got cold stares from them) and knelt next to the Messiah. She took the first step to becoming a worshiper.

Jesus said that Mary had chosen "the one thing" that was necessary. This one thing was the act of worship. When all is said and done, when we have labored, prayed, served, preached, given and served again, worship is our priority. It should be the first thing we do when we wake up, and the last thing we do when our heads hit our pillows at night. Worship is where we find our true identities. When we kneel in worship—humbling ourselves before God and acknowledging His rule over our lives—we discover why we were created. Our focus becomes most clear when we look at Him.

And, thus, began Mary's journey of worship. With the approval of the Master, it did not matter if Martha was upset or if Jesus' other disciples were angry that she busted up the Good Ole Boys' Club. She was hooked. She became a passionate follower of the Savior.

Yet we all know that it is not how you start this journey of faith; it is how you end it. Many people who fall in love with Jesus lose the excitement when they encounter the tests, trials and delays that distract and sidetrack us. What Jesus wants from us is consistency. He invites us to have the courage to worship Him no matter what is going on around us. The gospels show us a second scene in Mary's life where her faith was tested dramatically.

Tormented by Doubt

When Mary and Martha sent news to Jesus that their brother, Lazarus, was about to die, Jesus did not respond the way His friends expected. He actually snubbed their request. When Jesus heard that Lazarus was sick, "He then stayed two days longer in the place where He was" (John 11:6). For Mary and Martha, those were two very long days.

Doubts tormented them. What kind of friend was Jesus, anyway? Why did He ignore their urgent plea? Why did He not drop everything and rush to their aid? Mary was especially frustrated and distraught about Jesus' seemingly insensitive action.

When Jesus finally arrived in Bethany—four days after Lazarus died—a shroud of gloom covered the village. Everybody was in mourning. Mary was overwhelmed with grief and disappointment. Her faith was as cold as Lazarus's corpse. Mary did not even want to talk to Jesus.

This woman, who was known as a passionate disciple of the Lord, stayed in the house when her sister went outside to meet Jesus and express her own sorrow at His absence (see verse 20). We do not know what Mary was doing in the house. Most likely she was sulking, maybe even struggling with feelings of anger toward Jesus.

The worshiper, in this instance, had hit a wall. The woman who had been so enthusiastic about her newfound faith in Jesus now felt puzzled, and maybe even betrayed. Is He who He really says He is? Can she still trust Him?

You may relate to Mary. Many of us get stuck in this place of disillusionment. We get upset when God does not work according to our timetables. Perhaps you have been asking Jesus to intervene in your crisis. You may need Him to rescue a wayward child, heal your body, provide for a financial need, restore a broken relationship or salvage a dream that is on its deathbed. It may seem that Jesus has missed His golden opportunity—or that He was so busy meeting the needs of others that He just dropped you from His priority list.

Like Mary of Bethany, you may feel that Jesus waited too long. Your problem is now so serious, and your dream so lifeless, that Jesus cannot help you. When we face these frustrating delays, we automatically assume that He is denying us, neglecting us or rejecting us. So we throw a pity party. We go into our rooms, close our doors, shut out the pain and stay as far away from Jesus as possible.

Most of us find it too difficult to pray when we are in a faith crisis. The enemy of our souls tells us that Jesus does not care, that our prayers are meaningless and that there is no reward for believing in Him. Some of us, if we have melancholy tendencies, also beat ourselves up with the familiar "I guess I just don't have enough faith" line.

Mary did not stay in this self-made prison of depression. The Bible says that when Jesus neared the village, when He got close enough to Lazarus's tomb to smell the stench, He called for her, and Mary ran to him and fell at His feet—the place where she began her journey of discipleship. After all the questions, she set aside the blame games and returned to the only place where life's struggles made sense.

She decided to grow up. She left behind the whining immaturity that demanded Jesus must act a certain way. She put her trust in Him afresh, letting go of selfish expectations. When she surrendered her life to Him that day, she was saying that she would follow Him not only in the good times but also on the darkest days when she could not see His love through the clouds of suffering, pain and death.

There, at Jesus' feet, Mary caught a glimpse of Jesus that she had never seen before. He wept for His friend Lazarus, and then He commanded the lifeless body to come out of the tomb. Mary would have missed the miracle if she had stayed in seclusion. She needed to see with her own eyes that God's delays are not denials—and that Jesus' timing is perfect even when it seems He has forgotten us.

Press into His Presence

Do you relate to Mary? Do you feel as if Jesus has ignored your requests? Does it seem as if your message to Him was intercepted? Have you been sinking into discouragement because your dream has died—and Jesus does not care?

I encourage you to run back to Him and take your place at His feet. Return to the place of worship. True disciples know that life operates on God's schedule, not ours. Worship is not just for the good times. You must press through your doubts, surrender your deadlines, renounce your impatience and renew your trust in the Lord, who is the sovereign Lord over your circumstances. Ultimately, you must choose to make your home at His feet.

Mary of Bethany learned to do this. She appears in one other scene in the gospels, and, like the other two, she is shown kneeling at the feet of Jesus. In John 12, we are told that she took a pound of costly nard and rubbed the perfume on His feet with her hair—in much the same way that the sinful woman had done when Jesus was with Simon. Judas complained about the cost of Mary's act of worship (he was about to sell Jesus for thirty pieces of silver), but she did not defend her actions. She said nothing. All she did was worship.

Then Jesus defended Mary and made a profound statement about her in John 12:7: "Let her alone, so that she may keep it for the day of My burial." In Mark's account of this scene, Jesus said this:

> "Let her alone; why do you bother her? She has done a good deed to Me. . . . She has done what she could; she has anointed My body beforehand for the burial. Truly I say to you, wherever the gospel is preached in the whole world, what this woman has done will be spoken of in memory of her."
>
> Mark 14:6, 8–9

Mary was not performing a religious duty here. She did not just decide to waste her family's supply of nard on Jesus so He would smell good. Unlike the male followers of Jesus, Mary understood what Jesus was about to do on the cross. She knew He was about to die, but she also understood that He was going to take the sins of the world upon Himself. She knew He was the Christ, the Lamb of God. And this revelation drove her to worship Him in an extravagant way.

This is why Jesus was so taken with her devotion—not just because she knelt at His feet, but also because she understood His identity and His mission. She was worshiping Him in spirit and in truth. True worship is not just about emotional display, although you may certainly overflow with emotions. True worship is not just about getting goose bumps in a church meeting, or feeling warm and fuzzy, although God's presence certainly can evoke strong feelings.

Worship, if it is genuine, will always lead into a deeper revelation of the Lord. Those who choose to sit at His feet should buckle their seat belts, because He is going to take them on a thrilling journey of discovery. It may be fraught with disappointments and delays; it may be downright scary at times. But in the end, if we fix our gaze on Him, we will receive the same reward that Mary of Bethany received: an intimate understanding of who Christ really is.

Notice that Mary's worship in the third scene was also highly extravagant. Some Bible scholars believe that the pound of nard she "wasted" on Jesus was worth a year's wages in that primitive economy.[8] Others have speculated that the perfume represented Mary's dowry, and that she sacrificed it all in a moment of unbridled devotion.[9]

There is a message in the cost of that ointment. Jesus is calling women of God today to be radical worshipers. He wants you to cast aside all inhibitions, all fears of what others will think of your faith. This does not mean you have to stand on your head the next time you go to church, or do cartwheels down the aisle. But are you willing to worship with all your heart, soul, mind and strength?

I was raised in a sophisticated church; unless we were holding up our hymnals, we kept our hands by our sides. No one dared say "Amen!" during the sermon lest others think he was a religious fanatic. But right before I went to college, I had a life-changing experience with the Holy Spirit (which I will talk more about in chapter 14) and began to hang around with charismatic Christians. I had never known about such people.

I was shocked when I went to my first charismatic church event and saw people manifesting their passion for God. They clapped, shouted, danced, swayed, raised their hands, waved their arms and sang with vibrancy. But their excitement was contagious, and I caught it. I learned to overcome my reservations, and I became a passionate worshiper.

If you take this bold step, I can promise that people will criticize you. It may be friends or family members. Like Judas, they will accuse you of wasting your life. They will say God does not need or require such lavish praise. Do not listen to the critics. Tune out the voices that are urging you to play it safe. Mary of Bethany said nothing when Judas complained about her worship—she just went right on pouring her perfume on the Lord.

I encourage you to become a courageous worshiper. Never mind who is watching. Take your focus off your problems. Lose yourself in Him in total abandonment. Open your alabaster box and lavish your praise on the Savior.

LET'S TALK ABOUT IT

1. Why was it so significant that Mary of Bethany sat at Jesus' feet and listened to His Word (see Luke 10:38–42)? Why was this a revolutionary act?
2. Mary struggled when Jesus did not come quickly to help Lazarus. But ultimately she came back to Jesus and knelt at His feet once more. Describe a time when you got angry or were disappointed with God. How did you resolve it?
3. In John 12:1–8, Mary is shown kneeling at Jesus' feet a third time. Why did she pour the perfume on Him?
4. God wants us to be uninhibited in our worship. Have you ever been criticized for being too demonstrative in worship? Or do you find it difficult to express your emotions in worship?

A MESSAGE FROM YOUR HEAVENLY FATHER

My precious daughter,

I have called you to live in My presence. I created you to have an intimate relationship with Me. I want to spend time with you. I want to reveal Myself to you, through My Word and through My Spirit speaking to your heart. I want you to be in My presence at all times, not just when everything is going right. I want you to sit at My feet when you are discouraged, anxious, frustrated, angry or just weary. If you will worship Me in the difficult moments, I will give you new strength. Don't be afraid to sing, dance and shout in My presence. If you pour out your heart in worship, the cares of this life will grow dim. And as you gaze at Me, I will remove the veil and reveal My glory to you.

12

The Samaritan Woman

The Courage to Forgive

If I feel bitterly toward those who condemn
me . . . forgetting that if they knew me as I know
myself they would condemn me much more, then
I know nothing of Calvary's love.

—Irish missionary Amy Carmichael (1867–1951),
who founded the Dohnavur Mission for girls in India

We call her "the woman at the well" because the gospel of
John does not reveal her name. We are not told the identities of her five husbands or why they divorced her. In the days
of Jesus, a man could divorce his wife for any number of trivial
reasons—such as burning his dinner. This pitiful woman, who
was likely very poor, was probably a social outcast as well. This
explains why she came to the well at the hottest time of the day—a
time when others would be avoiding the scorching sun.

Yet on a particular morning this troubled woman had a head-on collision with her destiny when she met an unlikely visitor who was sitting by the well she visited daily. She was shocked to see a man sitting there, and probably embarrassed. She would have been even more surprised when Jesus initiated a conversation with her, and then shifted it to a serious theological discussion. No other rabbi in Israel would have done that, since rabbis did not talk to women in public—especially about spiritual matters. The Bible says in John 4:7–9:

> There came a woman of Samaria to draw water. Jesus said to her, "Give Me a drink." For His disciples had gone away into the city to buy food. Therefore the Samaritan woman said to Him, "How is that you, being a Jew, ask me for a drink since I am a Samaritan woman?" (For Jews have no dealings with Samaritans.)

She came with her cumbersome water pot on her head, the heaviness of her load symbolizing the weighty emotional burden she carried. She was full of rejection and disappointment. We have little information about her history—only that she had been passed from one man to the next over the course of her adult life. Her self-worth was in shambles. Yet here was a prime candidate to receive the Messiah's love. When Jesus ventured into Samaritan territory that day, He went as an evangelist to win this woman's soul.

We cannot fully appreciate the Samaritan woman's story without understanding the place where it occurred. John 4:5–6 tells us that Jesus came to a city of Samaria called Sychar, "near the parcel of ground that Jacob gave his son Joseph; and Jacob's well was there." These words are linked to a passage in Genesis 33:18–20, where we find that Jacob, centuries earlier, bought land for "one hundred pieces of money" (verse 19). One of the saddest tragedies in the Bible occurred on this land.

In Genesis 34, we read that Dinah, the beautiful daughter of Jacob and Leah, wandered into Canaanite territory without any clue that she was stepping into a nightmare. She was not dressed provocatively or looking for trouble. Yet her innocence was stolen that day when Shechem, a local prince, raped her (see Genesis 34:1–2). We never hear Dinah's screams or muffled sobs. In fact, we never hear the voice of Dinah again in Scripture. Shechem tried to bargain for her hand in marriage after he stole her virginity, but Jacob's sons plotted to kill him and his brothers for his act of defilement.

Yet the bloody act of revenge did not bring healing or restoration to Dinah. She was most likely shut away for the rest of her life, since women who had been raped in those days were considered unclean and unmarriageable. The attack was not her fault—but she bore the guilt. She lived the rest of her life sequestered in shame.

Dinah's silence in Genesis 34 is deafening. She represents the tragic loss of innocence endured by all women who have been sexually or physically abused, who have been violated and then blamed and shamed for crimes they did not commit.

What is most intriguing about Dinah's story is its setting. It occurred on a dusty plot of ground that would later become part of Samaria. We do not read much more in the Bible about that awful place until the Son of God arrived there to speak with the woman at the well.

It is truly amazing that Jesus was willing to visit that defiled site. During the days of His ministry, no rabbi in Israel would dare go near it. Rabbis took the long road around Samaria to avoid mixing with its people. They did not like Samaritans, and the feeling was mutual. Jews considered Samaritans racial half-breeds, and they did not like their hybrid religion either.

Yet the Bible says Jesus marched right into Samaria and sat down at Jacob's well, waiting for a divine appointment with a battered, bruised, nameless woman. In the same location where Dinah was raped centuries earlier, Jesus broke every religious rule in Jewish rabbinical tradition by conversing with this dejected woman in a public place.

After He spoke tenderly to the Samaritan woman, telling her of the water of life that comes from the true Messiah, He looked into her tormented soul and drained out the pain she had endured from men who had misused her. But to heal the pain, He had to lance the boil. He had to probe. He asked her about the most painful issue in her life.

"Go, call your husband and come here," Jesus told her. She threw up her defenses and protested, saying that she did not have a husband. Jesus replied: "You have correctly said, 'I have no husband'; for you have had five husbands, and the one whom you now have is not your husband" (John 4:16–18).

Jesus was not wagging His finger in the woman's face or condemning her behavior. No, He was making it obvious that He understood her life story. She had been mistreated and abandoned by five men in a row, and by the time the last man threw her out of the house she had no self-esteem left. The sixth man did not even have the decency to marry her.

Six men. Six painful scars. Yet on that day in Samaria, the dark clouds that had cast a heavy pall over all women in that region parted. *The seventh man had arrived!* Jesus was willing to go to this forsaken place—and identify with the pain of abused women. He offered the Samaritan woman not only total freedom from her guilt—but also the boldness to share her story of redemption with an entire village at a time when women did not speak in public.

Do you see the amazing mercy of God at work here? Jesus answered Dinah's cry. The world—and often the Church—is rarely willing to visit the place of abuse. Like the self-righteous rabbis who refused to step on Samaritan soil, many religious leaders today are unwilling to broach publicly the topic of domestic violence or sexual abuse. We sweep the pain under a rug and ignore the victims, so they hobble around the arid landscape cloaked in shame and weighed down by their heavy loads.

But Jesus, our compassionate Savior, broke both cultural and religious rules to bring His miraculous healing to this forsaken place. He headed straight for the heart of the issue, stood on the ground where Dinah had suffered, and announced freedom. He found a woman who bore the same shame Dinah did. And there, sitting next to the well of Jacob, He poured His miraculous healing into her heart and set her spirit free. Today, He will do the same for any woman who has been abused.

Dinah's Global Cry

Since 2001 I have traveled all over the world to share the healing of Christ with abused women in various cultures. Everywhere I go, whether it is in Asia, Latin America, the Middle East, Africa, Europe or in the comfortable suburbs of the United States, I hear Dinah's silent cry. When I remind these women of the Savior's love, and how He can heal their pain, they put down their heavy burdens and discover the same empowerment that the Samaritan woman did when she ran into her village and preached to all the men of the city. Jesus loves to turn mistreated women into evangelists!

The oppression of women is a global phenomenon, but it is manifested in different ways, depending on cultural factors. Here are a few of my own observations:

- In India, where boys are favored over girls, poor families sometimes kill girl babies because they do not want to have to pay the dowry for them when they grow up and get married. When girls do marry, their husbands typically abuse them physically. Women sometimes jump off bridges to kill themselves because they have no way to escape the abuse.

- In Uganda, where polygamy is legal and common, women feel inferior. They are expected to bow before their husbands to show honor, and up to 70 percent of women experience physical or sexual abuse.[1] (There is not even a word for "domestic violence" in the Buganda language.) A large percentage of Ugandan women are also abandoned, and then they are forced to feed their families with no financial help from their deadbeat husbands.

- In one region of South Africa that I visited in 2008, AIDS-infected men buy young girls to be their wives because they believe they can be cured of the virus if they have sex with a virgin.

- In Nigeria, widows are often evicted from their homes and thrown into the streets, and relatives sometimes blame them for their husbands' deaths. Also, men demand that their wives give birth to sons—and if they do not, they sometimes divorce them (not realizing, of course, that it is the man's sperm that determines the sex of the child).

- In regions of Latin America, women suffer serious beatings regularly in their homes. The *machismo* culture says that men are superior, and that women must spend their lives in subservience. In rural Guatemala, where I have ministered many times, it is typical to see a woman carrying a hundred-pound load of wood on her back while her husband walks twenty feet in front of her. He considers his wife to be nothing more than a pack animal. In Bolivia, poor indigenous women have a maxim that is known throughout the country; they say of their husbands: "The more he beats me, the more he loves me."

Abuse leaves serious emotional scarring. Women who have suffered from repeated sexual abuse, for example, can become emotional paralytics; they lack the resolve to function normally because they feel so worthless and inferior. Often they plunge into depression, which easily leads into addiction to prescription medicines. One depressed woman I prayed for, who was abused by a male relative for years, told me: "I have always felt like damaged goods."

In many of my healing conferences, I call several men to the platform and ask them to kneel on the stage in view of the women in the audience. I ask the women not to close their eyes, but to look at the men and imagine that they represent the men who have hurt them—whether those men were abusive husbands, deadbeat fathers, sexual predators, selfish boyfriends who stole their virginity, fathers who never showed affection or pastors who squelched their spiritual gifts. (It is not unusual to pray with women who have been raped or molested by pastors.)

Then I ask the men on the platform to pray. Standing in the gap for the men who perpetrated the abuse, these men ask God for forgiveness. Almost every time I do this, the women begin to cry as the Holy Spirit sweeps over the room and begins to heal hearts. They cannot believe that men are actually apologizing for the pain they cause, and this opens the door for a rush of forgiveness from the women. Before the meeting is over, the pain of abuse is drained and hearts are healed.

If you have been battered physically or verbally, molested, abandoned, raped or emotionally abused, your pain is real. You are not making it up, and it was not your fault. But in order to find healing, you must have the courage to bring your pain into the light of Christ. You cannot live in denial. Do not hide it or pretend it is not there. You must face this monster, but you do not have to face it alone. God can carry you through the process of healing, and He will send people into your life to pray for you every step of the way.

When Jesus asked the Samaritan woman about her husband, He was challenging her to face her pain. At that point she stood at a crossroads: She could face the truth, or she could walk away from the well and ignore Jesus. His strategy worked. Jesus showed her that even though she had a painful past, and even though so many men had hurt her, His love could restore.

Her response was swift. She ran into her village and told all the men, "Come, see a man who told me all the things that I have done" (John 4:29). This was a courageous step for the Samaritan woman, considering that her five former husbands and her live-in partner were probably in the crowd. Any woman who has experienced the healing of Jesus discovers a new boldness! Because she had just encountered the love of the Savior, she did not care about people's reactions. She had faced her pain. She was free.

The Samaritan woman became one of the first women to be ordained by Jesus. She became a preacher herself. The impact of her words was not minimal: John 4:39 says that "many of the Samaritans believed in Him because of the word of the woman who testified, 'He told me all the things that I have done.'" The story continues in verses 40-42:

> So when the Samaritans came to Jesus, they were asking Him to stay with them; and He stayed there two days. Many more believed because of His word; and they were saying to the woman, "It is no longer because of what you said that we believe, for we have heard for ourselves and know that this One is indeed the Savior of the world."

This is one of the earliest recorded instances of mass evangelism in Scripture, and it is the first time non-Jews recognized Jesus as the Messiah. And what triggered this miracle was an abused woman's healing. Just as Peter received the keys to the Kingdom, and Mary Magdalene was allowed to be the first to testify of the resurrection of Christ, this unnamed woman had the privilege of opening the door for the Gospel in Samaria. She did not run away when Jesus put His finger on her pain. Instead, she allowed His compassion to restore her bleeding heart.

Healing Can Be Yours

Abused women are plagued with self-doubts and barraged by negative accusations. Because of shame, the lies are many:

- "You deserved to be abused because you are a bad person."
- "He abused you because you wanted him to. You are responsible for his bad behavior."
- "Now that this has happened to you, you are worthless. Nothing good can ever happen to you now. Your life is ruined."
- "God cannot use you now. You've been stained forever."

All these statements are false, but if you have ever believed any one of them, you must face it bravely and apply the Word of God to your tormented mind. You must stop agreeing with the negative voices and choose to believe the truth.

One of the most common lies is that God cannot use you because you were abused. That is laughable. Many women whom God is using today have abusive backgrounds. One of them is Bible teacher Joyce Meyer, whose books and television broadcasts are reaching people all over the world.

You may think Meyer is the poster girl for success because she preaches to huge crowds, has sold millions of books and funds countless compassion projects in poor countries. But you may not know that her father abused her for fifteen years, and that her reaction to the trauma made her angry, rebellious and hateful toward men.

She left her abusive home at eighteen and soon entered a painful marriage. She and her first husband separated twenty times in five years, and he abandoned her twice. She was forced to live in a small rooming house (eating bologna sandwiches, cupcakes and Pepsi, she admits), until her husband finally deserted her.[2]

Yet God had big plans for Meyer. She eventually met Dave Meyer, a Christian man whom she married in 1967. Nine years later the Lord spoke to her and said, *You are going all over the place to teach My Word*. She began her teaching ministry with a Bible study at her church in suburban St. Louis, and 115 people came to the first one.[3] Today, she teaches millions of people how to break free from worry, bitterness, strife and selfishness so they can experience the abundant life of Christ.

At one point in her life, in her shame and pain, Meyer resembled the woman at the well. But the transforming power of Jesus changed everything. The same can be true for you. If you have been abused, here are some simple steps to finding freedom from the pain of abuse:

1. *Turn to Jesus Christ*. Jesus cares about women. During His ministry on earth He healed them, defended them publicly from accusation and affirmed women who were outcasts. Some of His most passionate followers were His women disciples. You must realize that Jesus cares about you and wants to heal your pain.

2. *Stop blaming yourself.* Many women who were sexually abused as children grow up believing that they did something sinful to trigger the abuse. Women who have suffered beatings or other forms of domestic cruelty are sometimes told that the abuse would never have happened if they had been "more submissive." These are all lies. God does not blame you for the actions of others. Renounce any lies you have believed that say you are the cause of someone else's behavior.

3. *Tune out negative voices.* Abuse can strip us of human dignity and self-worth. Many abused women have been subjected to continual verbal assaults: They have been told they are ugly, fat, stupid, useless, hopeless and so on. God does not think those things about you. If you get to know the Lord, and read His Word, He will change the way you view yourself.

Stop playing these negative recordings over and over in your mind, and instead meditate on the words of Scripture. Believe what God says about you:

- You are loved, and you are His precious daughter.
- Jesus paid the ultimate price to redeem you because you are valuable to Him.
- He will never leave you or forsake you.
- He will rescue you from your enemies.
- He will give you beauty for your ashes, and He will change your heaviness into praise.

4. *Forgive.* No matter what was done to you, you must forgive your abuser from your heart. Do not let anger, resentment or

bitterness ruin your life. Unforgiveness is toxic: If you allow anger to seethe inside of you, it will poison your emotions, twist your personality, harm your body and infect people around you.

Let go of the hurt now. I invite you to pray this prayer:

Father, You know that _____ *hurt me.* [It is important for you to say the name or names aloud.] *You know that what he did to me was not right. But I choose today to forgive him. I relinquish all desire to see him punished. I ask instead that You extend Your mercy to him. Don't give him what he deserves, but reach out to him and forgive his sins—just as You have forgiven mine. In Jesus' name, Amen.*

--- LET'S TALK ABOUT IT ---

1. John 4:1–42 describes Jesus' encounter with the Samaritan woman. Why is the location of this meeting so significant? What does it reveal to us about Jesus when we learn that He went to the place where Dinah was raped (see Genesis 34)?
2. Why was it so unusual for Jesus to go to Samaria and begin a conversation with a woman? What does this say to you about Jesus?
3. Women suffer various forms of oppression throughout the world. Have you seen evidence of "Dinah's silent cry"?
4. Why is it essential that we forgive those who abused or mistreated us?
5. Is there a painful experience in your past that you have not had the courage to face? Share this with your group and ask for prayer.

—— A MESSAGE FROM YOUR HEAVENLY FATHER ——

My precious daughter,

When My Son went to Samaria, He walked into a place of pain and fully engaged with the woman at the well. I will do the same for you. You can give Me all your pain, and I will take it from you. Even though many people ignore the pain women experience, I do not. I understand your emotional trauma. I hear the cry of all those who suffer at the hands of others. I sent My only begotten Son into the world so He could identify with your pain. He took it to the cross so you could be healed. Come to the well. The water I give you will become in you like a well of water springing up to eternal life. As I heal your heart, the healing waters of My Spirit will flow from you to others, and they will be healed as well.

13

Mary Magdalene, Witness of Christ's Resurrection

The Courage to Go First

The very first person to be commissioned was a woman. And she was commissioned to go to men to share her testimony . . . and then also to give His Word. I know there are some people who will draw a line and say I can give a testimony, but I can't share the Scripture. But Jesus didn't make that distinction. He gave Mary Magdalene both commissions, to share her testimony and to give out His word.

—Bible teacher Anne Graham Lotz, daughter of evangelist Billy Graham

Barb Becker is a tough lady from Western stock. Raised by alcoholic parents in a mining camp in Wyoming, she lived a rough life that included drugs and promiscuity. People continually told her she was good for nothing. She hated herself and became suicidal. "I was the woman with seven devils," Barb told me, echoing the Bible's description of Mary Magdalene.

But in 1985, on the same day she planned to kill herself, she bought a paperback book called *Power for Living* for 25 cents at a secondhand store, read the Christian testimonies in it and prayed to receive Jesus as her Savior. She became so hungry to know God that she read the Bible straight through four times in three months and ended up getting baptized with the Holy Spirit. Barb now pastors Glory of the Lord Family Ministries, a small charismatic church in Watford City, North Dakota.

It was not an easy journey for this tough-as-leather cowgirl. When some church leaders encouraged her back in the 1990s to consider a pastoral position, she dismissed the thought. Despite the fact that she was a trailblazer—she was one of the first women in North Dakota to drive trucks for the oil industry—she did not feel qualified to be a pastor.

But God challenged Barb's attitudes in May 2000 when she attended a conference in Saskatchewan, Canada. A Nigerian pastor, Femi Ogunrinde, issued a call for people to come to the altar if they were not sure of their spiritual callings. As Barb stood at the stage with her eyes closed, she thought to herself: *Lord, I can't do this. I'm a woman.*

Ogunrinde then said into the microphone: "Some of you are telling God you cannot fulfill your calling because you are a woman."

That got Barb's attention, but she continued her silent argument. *Lord, I can't be a pastor. I haven't been to Bible college or seminary.*

Ogunrinde then said, as if on cue: "Some of you have disqualified yourselves because you haven't been to Bible college or seminary."

Barb was starting to feel emotionally vulnerable at this point. Her protest continued: *But Lord, my husband is not where he should be with You.*

The Nigerian preacher responded again from the stage: "Some of you have said you cannot be a leader because your husband is not serving God."

Barb was aware that God was doing painful surgery as He challenged every one of her excuses. Next she thought of her conservative Lutheran community: *But Lord, You know I can't do this in Watford City.*

Ogunrinde challenged her again. "Some of you are saying, 'Lord, I cannot serve You in this way because of the place where I live.'"

At that point Barb began sobbing. She let go and surrendered to the call. When she got back to her seat, a friend poked her with her elbow and said: "Do you get it now?"

Barb was ordained in August 2001 and has pastored her church since then. It is not an easy job for a woman. Some people have actually shunned her. When I ministered in Barb's church in 2010, she told me horror stories of discrimination and ridicule. Christians have told her she is "in rebellion," either because she teaches from the pulpit or because her husband is not in ministry with her. "They don't realize that I couldn't do what I do without my husband's full support," Barb told me.

The beautiful scenery of North Dakota reminded me that much of the American West was pioneered by courageous women like Barb Becker who defied stereotypes and broke molds. When Congress passed the Homestead Act of 1862, which offered free land to people willing to settle it, many women accepted the offer (years before they could vote) and endured incredible hardship to carve out farms and ranches in arid areas. They were willing to lead.

A Woman with Apostolic Grace

One of the reasons Barb Becker struggled with the idea of pastoring a church is because our culture, both secular and religious, tells us that women are not initiators. Tradition says men are out front while women are in the background; men are vocal while women are quiet; men are leaders and women are followers. And sometimes we read these cultural biases into the Bible.

Suppose I ask, for example, "Who were the first followers of Jesus?" I always get the same answer: "Peter, James, John and Andrew." We even associate the word *disciples* with men. We assume that all of Christ's original entourage was a boys' club. While it is true that He appointed twelve Jewish males to minister alongside Him, the Bible never suggests that He excluded women. We are told of Jesus in Luke 8:1–3:

> Soon afterwards, He began going around from one city and village to another, proclaiming and preaching the kingdom of God. The twelve were with Him, and also some women who had been healed of evil spirits and sicknesses: Mary who was called Magdalene, from whom seven demons had gone out, and Joanna the wife of Chuza, Herod's steward, and Susanna, and many others who were contributing to their support out of their private means.

This is a fascinating angle on Jesus' ministry, and one that many people miss because of their own biases. Jesus was revolutionary when it came to attitudes about the sexes. Not only did He have women followers, but some of them were quite prominent, and they played a vital role in furthering Jesus' ministry: They were paying the bills! Joanna, Susanna and the rest of these women were not just making sandwiches or washing clothes for the men on Jesus' team. They were learning from Him, supporting Him and fulfilling the role of ministry partners.

This was especially true of the woman known as Mary Magdalene. Scholars know little about her, other than the fact that she was from a region called Magdala. Some have typecast her as a prostitute, but the Bible never describes her as such. (And Scripture never even remotely suggests that Jesus had a sexual relationship with her, as the popular book *The Da Vinci Code* purports.)

What we do know, from Luke 8, is that Mary Magdalene was delivered of seven demons after spending time with Jesus. She was a transformed woman. Since seven is a biblical number of completion, I believe Mary Magdalene was completely free. She was not halfway delivered. She had such a powerful encounter with the Savior, and knew Him in such a close, personal way, that she was free from all the baggage of her past.

The Bible does not give us details about the demons that plagued Mary Magdalene. She could have been an idol worshiper or entangled in witchcraft. She could have been immoral and plagued by the sexual shame. If she suffered abuse, her soul could have been a nest of demonic activity including depression, self-hatred and resentment. We do not know the specifics of her past sins, but we do know that she was fully delivered.

In my travels around the world I have ministered to women who were bound by demonic spirits. Once when I was in northern India, in the city of Patna, a thin woman in a yellow sari came to the altar when we gave an invitation for people to receive the salvation of Christ. I could tell immediately that this lady had a problem: Her face began to twitch, she was breathing heavily, and her eyes began rolling into the back of her head. Then, as she drew closer to the altar, she began sticking out her tongue and flicking it from side to side. Her tongue began protruding farther and farther out of her mouth until she looked like a snake!

I grabbed a friend of mine named Maureen and we took this woman to the back of the church so she would not distract everyone else. We knew she had a demon (we later learned she was a Hindu witch), but she sincerely wanted to give her life to Jesus. The devils inside her were putting up a fight.

This woman was terrified of the demons that were manifesting inside her, so Maureen and I stroked her arm to reassure her. Then we quietly but forcefully commanded the spirits to let go of her. The deliverance did not happen instantaneously, but within fifteen minutes she was free—and smiling because she also prayed to ask Jesus to come into her heart. This woman's tormented face was transformed in front of our eyes. By the end of the morning she was beaming.

I imagine this is the type of transformation that happened in Mary Magdalene's life so long ago. Jesus had lifted her burden completely. She was no longer depressed, anxious, sick, resentful or ashamed. She was 100 percent delivered. And she was probably eager to tell everyone about the Messiah. People who have had dramatic encounters with the Lord are usually the most vocal about Him.

What is fascinating about Mary Magdalene is the strategic role she is allowed to play in the Gospel story. Even though she lived in a culture dominated by men, she is portrayed in the Bible as the first person to announce the resurrection of Jesus. This honor was not given to Peter, James or John—none of the three who saw Jesus transfigured with Moses and Elijah or who accompanied Him in the Garden of Gethsemane. The first person to be commissioned by the Lord Himself to carry the Good News of the Gospel was this beloved female follower, Mary Magdalene, who had experienced His resurrection power in her own life.

The Easter story has many amazing scenes: Jesus' last Passover meal with His disciples, His arrest and brutal scourging, His crucifixion between two criminals and the dramatic darkness that fell on Jerusalem at the moment of His death. But my favorite part of the story is when Mary Magdalene peered into Jesus' tomb on that resurrection morning. John 20:11–12 describes it this way:

> But Mary was standing outside the tomb weeping; and so, as she wept, she stooped and looked into the tomb; and she saw two angels in white sitting, one at the head and one at the feet, where the body of Jesus had been lying.

The two angels were sitting at the head and foot of Jesus' grave. Does that image remind you of anything? These heavenly creatures bring to mind the carved cherubim that, facing each other, graced the lid of the Ark of the Covenant—the golden box that contained the holiest relics of Israel's history. Second Kings 19:15 tells us that God was "enthroned above the cherubim."

That ancient Ark was hidden behind a veil in the Tabernacle of Moses, and later King Solomon's Temple. Under the rules of the Old Covenant, the manifest presence of God was off limits. Sinful men and women had to stand at a distance, and only the high priest could enter the Holy of Holies once a year to make atonement. No one else was allowed to see God's glory as it blazed between the two angels.

Yet on Easter morning, after the Lamb of God had been sacrificed on Calvary's cross, the stone covering Christ's tomb was rolled away to reveal this profound sight. The two angels appeared on top of His grave to show us that the glory of God was now accessible to us. The Holy of Holies was no longer closed off. In the Temple, the veil was torn from top to bottom. Under the New Covenant, we can run to the mercy seat!

And who was the first to see this profound sight? Mary Magdalene—a woman who would have been considered an outcast by the religious community—got the first glimpse of this astounding revelation!

But there is so much more to discover in this account of Mary's encounter with the risen Christ. John 20 can be fully understood only if we compare it with the story of the Fall of man in Genesis 3. Notice the similarities:

1. *There were two gardens.* Man's Fall occurred in the Garden of Eden—a place of intimate fellowship with God. After Adam and Eve disobeyed Him, the Lord cursed the ground and banished them from Paradise. On Resurrection Sunday, Christ appeared in a garden (John 19:41 says Joseph of Arimathea donated a garden tomb to Jesus) to remind us that now, because of His redemption, intimate fellowship with God is available again. Jesus reopened the doors to Eden.

2. *There were two women.* Sin entered the world when a serpent deceived the first woman, Eve. On Resurrection Sunday, after Christ had defeated Satan through His atoning death, Jesus appeared first to a woman—one who had previously been in bondage to Satan's demons (see John 20:14). Mary Magdalene is the New Testament counterpart to Eve. Her life reminds us that Jesus offers us total deliverance from the bondage of our past.

3. *There were two gardeners.* In the story of the Fall, Eve and her husband, Adam, the tenders of Eden, rebelled against God after she was deceived. On Easter morning, Mary Magdalene met a man outside the tomb who she thought was a gardener. When she realized it was Jesus she exclaimed, "Rabboni!," and began to embrace Him. The woman in the second story is with Christ, "the last Adam . . . the second man" (1 Corinthians 15:45, 47). We now have this promise:

"For as in Adam all die, so also in Christ all will be made alive" (verse 22).

4. *There were two sets of angels.* After Adam and Eve fell into sin, God posted the cherubim with the flaming sword east of Paradise to keep mankind out (see Genesis 3:24). On Easter morning, two angels appeared in the garden, not to banish mankind from God's presence but to invite us to behold the risen Messiah.

Why are there so many parallels in these two stories? The Holy Spirit wants us to know that in God's great plan of redemption He unraveled Eden's curse. The death and resurrection of Jesus reversed the effects of the Fall. While Genesis 3 describes pain, slavery to sin and alienation from God's presence, John 20 reveals healing, deliverance and full restoration of fellowship with the Son of God.

Women: You Have Been Commissioned

Why did Jesus choose to reveal Himself to Mary Magdalene after His resurrection? Why did He send her forth to the brethren as the first witness of His Good News? What does all this mean for women today?

We begin to answer these questions by noting how Jesus again broke with tradition. In first-century Israel, women were not allowed to testify in a court of law: They were considered unreliable witnesses. Yet when Jesus was raised from the dead, and He wanted this fact proclaimed to the world, He first commissioned one of His women followers to spread the news.

Here are His words to Mary Magdalene:

Jesus said to her, "Stop clinging to Me, for I have not yet ascended to the Father; but go to My brethren and say to them, 'I ascend to

My Father and your Father, and My God and your God.'" Mary Magdalene came, announcing to the disciples, "I have seen the Lord," and that He had said these things to her.

John 20:17–18

I call this scene in John 20 "the great reversal." By using all this garden imagery from Eden on the morning of His resurrection, God made it clear that He was breaking the curse of sin that came on the earth after mankind's Fall. He was also saying that He has a new role for women to play in His plan.

Under the curse of sin, the woman—Eve—not only came under the bondage of sin in a general sense, but was placed at a disadvantage in her relationship with men. God told her that her husband would rule over her (see Genesis 3:16). She would know pain, oppression, abuse and heartache. And she would also lose her voice. After the Fall, women did not exercise the authority that Eve enjoyed in the Garden.

Through the redemption of Christ, the woman got her voice back. Mary Magdalene was appointed to go and tell. She was commissioned to preach. Jesus did not limit her, restrict her or tell her to stay out of the pulpit. Instead, He ordained her to be a carrier of His glorious Gospel.

Women are no longer to be subservient; they are no longer relegated to suffer in silence in the face of abuse; they are no longer expected to blend into the background. Jesus has now called women to be His missionaries and His preachers.

So why are women barred from leadership positions in many churches today? Since, as we have learned, women were actually free in the New Testament era to preach, prophesy, serve as deacons, pastor churches and exercise their spiritual gifts, why have conservative Christians placed restrictions on what women can do in ministry?

Put simply, women are not allowed to offer authoritative speech in church because Eve deceived Adam. The reasoning goes like this: Since the first woman led her husband into temptation, all women will do the same. Therefore, all women must remain under an eternal form of control and punishment for what Eve did in the Garden.

This line of reasoning, however, denies the power of redemption through Christ. If Jesus paid for our sins once and for all when He died on the cross, why, then, should women continue to suffer for the sin of the first woman? Again we see that it is a misrepresentation of Scripture to insist that Paul was forbidding women to hold positions of church leadership. Paul spent the entire book of Romans making it clear that all mankind has been forgiven through the atonement of Jesus. He did not go back to Ephesus and invent a new doctrine of female subjugation. All people, men and women, have been set free from the curse of sin.

This was dramatically illustrated on Easter morning, when Mary Magdalene was sent by Jesus to announce His Good News. Jesus did not pick Mary to be the first evangelist simply because she woke up earlier than the others that day. He was making it clear that, in Christ, there is "neither male nor female" (Galatians 3:28). He had restored the original authority given to man and woman in the Garden. Under the New Covenant, through the power of the Holy Spirit, both men and women can serve as ministers of His grace. And when He was raised from the dead, He commissioned His faithful disciple Mary Magdalene to blaze that trail for all women to follow.

─────────── LET'S TALK ABOUT IT ───────────

1. Many women, like Pastor Barb Becker, have resisted God's call on their lives simply because they are women. Have you ever told God you cannot do something because you are female? Share this story with your group.

2. Mary Magdalene was an unlikely candidate to be a disciple of Jesus because of her past. Are there things about your past that still haunt you and cause you to think you are disqualified from being used by God? If so, share these with your group and ask them to pray with you.

3. Compare the story of the Garden of Eden in Genesis 3 with the resurrection of Jesus in John 20. Why is this "the great reversal"?

4. Why is it so significant that, of all Jesus' early followers, He commissioned Mary Magdalene to be the first to tell of His resurrection?

―――― A MESSAGE FROM YOUR HEAVENLY FATHER ――――

My precious daughter,

I want to set you free completely. I did not send My Son to give you halfway deliverance, or three-quarters deliverance. Jesus made it possible for you to be totally free. When He paid the price for your sins at Calvary, He opened up a new and living way for you. The veil that separated us has been torn asunder. I invite you to spend time in My presence and know Me personally. When Jesus purchased your redemption, you received your voice back. It is now possible for you to stand in confidence and authority before Me—blameless, your sins forgiven. And because you are now restored to fellowship with Me, you are commissioned to speak for Me. You have permission to go first. Go and tell everyone about My love. Step out in confidence. I will be with you.

14

Priscilla, Spiritual Daughter of the Apostle Paul

The Courage to Mentor Others

Live in such a way as to pass something tangible
to a new generation.

—American missionary
Lillian Thrasher (1887–1961),
who established an orphanage in Egypt
in 1920 that still exists today

Henrietta Mears never looked the part of a trendy youth
speaker. In the 1940s and '50s, when her ministry to youth
was at its height, the dowdy chemistry teacher from Minnesota
would stand at her lectern at First Presbyterian Church of Hollywood, California, wearing thick glasses, a red dress and some
type of ornate hat. She was strict, had a disdain for tardiness and
spoke in a husky voice that commanded authority.

She did not entertain her pupils with fancy audiovisuals (this was long before the age of PowerPoint), yet crowds of five hundred or more students attended her Sunday school classes. By the early 1930s, during the time she served as Christian education director at her church, the ministry grew from four hundred to four thousand students. Later, when she began a summer Bible training ministry at the Forest Home Conference Center north of Los Angeles, she trained hundreds of future ministers.

Three of the most famous men who sat under Henrietta's ministry went on to lead millions to Jesus. One of them was evangelist Billy Graham. Another was Bill Bright, who founded Campus Crusade for Christ. The third was Dawson Trotman, founder of the Navigators discipleship ministry. All of these leaders considered Henrietta Mears a spiritual mother and mentor. Graham once said of her: "I doubt if any other woman outside my wife and mother has had such a marked influence on my life. She is certainly one of the greatest Christians I have ever known."[1]

Henrietta Mears was not satisfied to influence a few young people here and there. She was consumed with passion to teach the Bible to as many as possible, and to produce disciples who would in turn produce more disciples. One of the men she influenced, Presbyterian pastor Don Moomaw, later became the pastor of a Hollywood actor named Ronald Reagan. She also discipled Richard Halverson, who became chaplain of the United States Senate. Wherever she went, world-changing disciples were produced. Though she never married, her spiritual children, grandchildren and great-grandchildren are too numerous to count.

Mears was so passionate about training children in the truths of the Bible that she became the first publisher in the United States of a grade-level Sunday school curriculum. The Gospel Light Publishing Company, which she founded in 1933, continues to produce books and curricula for all ages, many years after her death in 1963. She knew intuitively that God would use her life like leaven to spread the Gospel farther than she could travel geographically. She told her students often of her world vision: "When I consider my ministry, I think of the world. Anything less than that would not be worthy of Christ, nor of his will for my life."[2]

I never got to sit in one of those uncomfortable wooden seats at Forest Home to listen to Miss Mears's Bible classes (although I have read her book *What the Bible Is All About*). But I have often wondered how this woman—who was old enough to be a grandmother to most of her students—had such a commanding influence on a generation. It certainly had nothing to do with her style; she dressed like a frumpy science teacher. Yet she captured the hearts of thousands of youth and imparted to them a love for the Bible.

The answer is that Miss Mears was not only a teacher, writer and publisher. Her passion for young people also made her an extraordinary mentor.

It takes courage to be a mentor, especially if you want to touch the younger generation. I know, because I had a Henrietta Mears in my life. When I was a senior in high school, I was attending a Baptist church in suburban Atlanta that was, as I have mentioned, quite traditional. The pastor taught the Bible, but sermons were limited to basic topics about salvation. I was not encouraged to go much deeper in my relationship with God.

But then I met June Leverette. She was a stay-at-home mother of two children who volunteered as a Sunday school teacher for the college-level class at my church. Since I was about to go to college, I joined the class and was immediately impressed with June's style. There was something unusual about her. When she opened her Bible I noticed she had verses underlined with colored markers on just about every page. She had also written many notes in the margins. And when she talked about Jesus in her thick Georgia drawl, I could tell she had a special relationship with Him.

I mentioned June's deep spirituality to a friend of mine, and he told me she was "charismatic." (It sounded like a disease to me!) My friend did not really know what the term meant, and this made me more curious. So after one Sunday morning session I worked up the courage to ask June about her charismatic experience. She smiled and said she would love to tell me about how she was baptized with the Holy Spirit—and she invited me to her home. I later learned that she wanted to meet offsite because the pastor had asked her not to talk about charismatic topics at the church.

When I visited June we sat in her paneled den. All around her chair were stacks of Christian books, as well as a concordance and several translations of the Bible. She had notebooks and journals full of her personal observations of Scripture, along with the many pens and colored pencils she used while studying. A cabinet near her chair was full of cassette tapes with sermons recorded by Bible teachers I had never heard of. The first thing I thought to myself when I saw it was, *Those Bible teachers are not Baptists!* My second observation was, *This lady is really serious about God!*

June sat in her chair for the next hour and shared how she had had a deep and personal experience with the Holy Spirit a few years earlier. She called it "the infilling" and "the baptism" with the Holy Spirit, and she flipped through various verses in the New Testament to make her point. She jumped from Luke to the book of Acts to 1 Corinthians, and then she handed me a book called *The Holy Spirit and You*, written by a man named Dennis Bennett. (I later learned he was an Episcopal priest who was baptized with the Holy Spirit in 1960.)

After our discussion I felt, like John Wesley, strangely warmed. I could sense my own spiritual hunger growing. I wanted what

June Leverette had because she made it so inviting. Growing up as a Southern Baptist, I knew what Jesus had done for me on the cross, and I understood His forgiveness. But no one had had ever talked to me about the work of the Holy Spirit. This was all new to me. I felt as if I had just stumbled into a whole warehouse full of new revelation, and I wanted to soak it all in.

I went home that day armed with the book by Bennett and several other volumes about the Spirit's supernatural power. For the next several days I read these voraciously, and reread the Scriptures that June had pointed out. Within a week I was ready to take the plunge. On a hot summer night in early September I sat down by myself on a concrete bench on the volleyball court outside my church and asked Jesus to baptize me with the Holy Spirit. He performed that miracle for me, and my life was changed. That experience forever marked my Christian life, empowered me for supernatural ministry and introduced me to segments of the Church that I never knew existed.

I stayed in close contact with June for several years. She continued to give me books to read and tapes to listen to; she also sent me letters of encouragement filled with Bible verses and prayers. Under her tutelage, I began to develop an intense hunger for God's Word. Before long, I was writing notes in the margins of my Bible, and underlining words and phrases in various colors. I did not realize what was happening at the time, but today it is obvious: June Leverette mentored me without my knowing it. She imparted her life. She modeled what it means to be a disciple, and led me into a deeper Christian experience than I had ever dreamed possible. A mother in her thirties had mentored a teenage boy—in a church where women were not allowed to engage in pulpit ministry!

As I have pondered my spiritual journey, and how God used June to prod me into baptism with the Holy Spirit, I am especially grateful that she stayed in our traditional church. She could have left years earlier in order to find a church that was more open to Spirit-filled ministry, but she chose to stay and invest in college students who might not otherwise encounter that experience. She had the courage to be a mentor, and to invest her life in others who needed a role model. That selfless decision ended up having an impact on one clueless teenager who became a leader in the Body of Christ many years later. I wonder how many other believers, young and old, could be mentored by mature Christian women who have so much to give.

Where Are the Priscillas?

When I read the book of Acts, I am reminded that the early Church was not built on religious structures and programs. Even though there were moments when crowds embraced the Gospel, ministry primarily took place between individuals. Jesus had told His followers before His ascension that they were to "go therefore and make disciples" (Matthew 28:19). Although Jesus Himself preached to crowds in public and performed miracles for the masses, the bulk of His ministry was spent with just a few select men and women who traveled with Him.

This is actually the way the Kingdom of God grows. Jesus invested in a few, and they in turn modeled Christ to their disciples— until thousands of Christians began spreading out beyond Jerusalem into the Roman world. After Paul was converted, he was discipled by the believers in Damascus and then by Barnabas. And eventually Paul began investing his life in a group of men and women who accompanied him on his missionary journeys. These people included Luke, the doctor who wrote one of the gospels; Timothy, his most trusted spiritual son; and a unique assortment of women who served in various ministry roles.

Paul often commended his spiritual daughters in his epistles. He praised Phoebe, a deacon and trusted emissary, in Romans 16:1–2. He encouraged Euodia and Syntyche, two women who probably led churches, in Philippians 4:1–3. But the woman most often mentioned in connection with Paul is Priscilla, a Roman woman who was married to a Jewish believer named Aquila.

Priscilla and Aquila ministered together as a couple, and they usually followed Paul on his journeys. Often they would stay behind and disciple the converts who had found Christ in an apostolic venture. They not only understood the fundamentals of the faith, but had the maturity necessary to give counsel and direction to fledgling churches in Asia Minor and Greece. Paul calls Priscilla and Aquila his "fellow workers" in Romans 16:3, and he points out that they "risked their own necks" for him—an obvious reference to persecution.

But the most poignant reference to Priscilla appears in the book of Acts, when she and Aquila are portrayed as spiritual mentors to a young and untested apostle named Apollos. Acts 18:24–26 says:

> Now a Jew named Apollos, an Alexandrian by birth, an eloquent man, came to Ephesus; and he was mighty in the Scriptures. This man had been instructed in the way of the Lord; and being fervent in spirit, he was speaking and teaching accurately the things concerning Jesus, being acquainted only with the baptism of John; and he began to speak out boldly in the synagogue. But when Priscilla and Aquila heard him, they took him aside and explained to him the way of God more accurately.

I am sure Aquila and Priscilla preached to crowds from time to time, but the Holy Spirit does not focus on the sensational aspects of ministry. In this case, we see a rather intimate moment when these spiritual parents came alongside a younger man and brought doctrinal clarity in a loving manner. The result? At the end of the narrative, we are told that Apollos "powerfully refuted the Jews in public, demonstrating by the Scriptures that Jesus was the Christ" (Acts 18:28). His ministry became ten times more effective because of the influence of godly mentors. One of them was a woman.

It is interesting that when Priscilla is mentioned in Scripture, her name is often listed before her husband's—even though in that culture the man's name would normally come first.[3] Scholars have long speculated that Priscilla was probably the more prominent teacher. One scholar, Ruth Hoppin, wrote a book called *Priscilla's Letter* in which she theorizes that Priscilla authored the book of Hebrews.[4] While that mystery may never be solved, it is certainly true that Priscilla had an impressive theological background. Her reputation in the primitive Church was that of a true spiritual mother and a passionate defender of the faith. She was one of the original torchbearers for the Gospel.

It is also true that she imparted her life. In the New Testament Church, older women were encouraged to teach younger women (see Titus 2:3–4), yet Priscilla did not limit her discipleship ministry to women. Like Henrietta Mears, she contributed to the development of male leaders of the Church.

Are you a Priscilla to someone else? Are you actively involved in discipling younger believers? You may need to take stock of how you are investing in relationships. I tell Christians they need three kinds of relationships in their lives:

1. *Pauls* are spiritual fathers and mothers you trust. All of us need older, wiser Christians who can guide us, pray for us and offer counsel. My mentors have encouraged me when I wanted to quit and propelled me forward when I lost sight of God's promises. In the journey of faith, you do not have

to feel your way in the dark. God gave Ruth a Naomi and Joshua a Moses. You can ask the Lord for a mentor if you do not have one.

2. *Barnabases* are spiritual peers who are bosom friends. They know everything about you, yet they love you anyway. They are also willing to rebuke you if necessary! They provide accountability in areas of personal temptation. And they will stay up all night praying for you when you face a crisis.

3. *Timothys* are the younger Christians you are helping to grow. Relational discipleship takes a lot of time and energy, but investing your life in others is one of the most fulfilling experiences in life. Once you have poured your life into another brother or sister, and watched him or her mature in Christ, you will never settle for superficial religion.

Jesus invested time in His disciples. He did not float about like a holographic Yoda while dispensing otherworldly wisdom. He hiked through Israel with His friends. They got their feet dirty together. He fished with them, ate with them and just hung out with them. Mark 3:14 says Jesus appointed the twelve "*so that they would be with Him* and that He could send them out to preach" (emphasis added). Notice that His relationship with them was not just about the task of ministry. He wanted their fellowship!

We sometimes get this backward. We tend to value religious performance, yet we are often bankrupt when it comes to friendships. We sit together in countless meetings, but never open our hearts to each other. Even ministers have admitted to me that they have no friends. We have created a robotic, "program-ized" Christianity that counts heads but lacks the heart of New Testament love.

I have learned that ministry is not about getting big crowds, filling seats, tabulating response cards or eliciting raucous applause. It is not about running on the church-growth treadmill. Religion that focuses on externals is performance-based. Our Gospel flows from the heart. Our faith is based on the astounding truth that a loving God came to earth to repair our broken relationship with Him. And since then, God has sent people across oceans and mountain ranges to tell others about His love.

Four Keys to Effective Mentoring

In 2010 I traveled to the nation of Colombia to preach in a conference sponsored by two churches in the city of Barranquilla. I could have gone alone, but I asked Jason, a young pastor from South Carolina, to accompany me on the ten-day trip. I did this because mentoring has become one of my core ministry values.

When we boarded our first flight to Panama I said to Jason: "You are going to grow two feet during this adventure." When we left Barranquilla ten days later, he told me: "I think I grew two-and-a-half feet." Nothing thrills me more than challenging young leaders like Jason by taking them on the mission field. I have done this in Nigeria, Ukraine, India, Peru, Bolivia, South Africa and other places. It is not always convenient to share a bathroom or double the travel costs, but the reward comes when I see how much the experience stretches their faith and accelerates their spiritual growth.

It is what many call the Timothy Principle, and it is found in Paul's words to his spiritual son in 2 Timothy 2:2: "The things which you have heard from me in the presence of many witnesses, entrust these to faithful men who will be able to teach others also."

Paul had discovered long before that the most effective way to expand the reach of the Gospel is to invest deliberately and personally in younger disciples. He always traveled with a small team; he shared his life with people such as Timothy, Silas, Phoebe, Lydia, Luke, Priscilla and Aquila—and they became spiritual giants. We would be wise to reclaim this forgotten art of personal discipleship.

Here are four guidelines I have developed for effectively training the next generation:

1. *Get on the same level.* One young leader I have been mentoring for a few years, Charles, once told a pastor that he wanted to be trained in ministry. The pastor explained that the training process would require Charles to carry the pastor's Bible, pick up his dry cleaning and serve as his chauffeur. The pastor did not offer to pray with Charles, take him on a ministry trip or share how to hear the voice of God or lead a sinner to salvation.

   Some pastors groom young leaders to be "armor bearers" who are nothing more than unpaid valets. I have seen some big-city bishops with celebrity entourages—including (literally) a guy to carry the preacher's Bible, another to carry his water bottle, another to carry his handkerchief and a fourth to fan him when he is sweating!

   This type of leader is infected with a virus known as *egotisticus giganticus*. He may call himself a "spiritual father" to these men, but they do not have access to his life. They might as well be his slaves. This is not biblical discipleship. Any real spiritual fathers or mothers will invite their disciples to get on their level and learn both the practical and spiritual sides of ministry.

2. *Be a genuine friend.* Young leaders today do not want simply to listen to a pastor's sermons or wait outside an office door until he or she asks them to fetch a cup of coffee. They crave relationships with humble, accessible men and women of

God who can model authentic Christianity. That requires plenty of one-on-one communication. True mentoring means inviting younger leaders into your life and letting them get up close and personal.

3. *Offer plenty of ministry opportunities.* Before I arrived in Colombia with Jason, I let my hosts know that he was available to speak in churches and youth meetings if they so desired. He ended up leading several powerful meetings with youth in the city. Then, on the last night, when I was addressing a group of leaders from two churches, I called Jason to come to the platform with me so he could pray and minister to people. I wanted Jason to be stretched in his faith.

   We will not effectively raise up younger leaders if we only allow them to carry our briefcases. They have to do the real stuff! I was so proud of Jason when he called several people to the front of the church and offered prophetic encouragement. The Colombians loved him, and the youth who had been in his meetings lined up to hug him when we left. In the end, Jason realized that he was a ministry partner with me, not just a trainee.

4. *Impart your life.* Young leaders today need to become effective communicators, and they must learn how to flow in the Holy Spirit's power. This means that we have to go beyond mere mechanics: We have to follow the apostle Paul's model. He told the Thessalonians: "Having so fond an affection for you, we were well-pleased to impart to you not only the gospel of God but also our own lives, because you had become very dear to us" (1 Thessalonians 2:8).

Discipleship requires sacrifice and genuine love. And it focuses on individuals. As much as I enjoy speaking to crowds, I have learned that often the most effective ministry in the Kingdom of God is to the one, not the multitude. Please do not ignore the younger believers you are called to encourage.

LET'S TALK ABOUT IT

1. Looking back on your spiritual journey, were there any spiritual mothers who mentored you, either directly or indirectly? Describe how they influenced you.

2. Henrietta Mears helped shape leaders such as Billy Graham and Bill Bright. Can you think of a time when you inspired or encouraged a younger person to excel spiritually? How did you do this?

3. Jesus commanded us to "make disciples." Why is relational discipleship more effective than just gathering crowds for large events?

4. Priscilla is a New Testament model of a spiritual mentor. Why is it so significant that the apostle Paul praised her in Scripture?

5. How could you be more proactive in helping to mentor younger believers?

A MESSAGE FROM YOUR HEAVENLY FATHER

My precious daughter,

I have called you to make disciples. The life of My Son is in you, and you can impart this life to others through teaching, encouragement, counsel and comfort. There are so many motherless and fatherless people who need what I have deposited in you. As you give to others, I will give to you. My wisdom and revelation will increase in you as you impart it to those you are discipling. Rise up and become the spiritual mother I have called you to be. Don't be intimidated by the needs and problems people face. I will give you the words to tell them each and every time. Freely you have received—now freely give to the people I have called you to touch.

15

The Four Daughters of Philip the Evangelist

The Courage to Speak for God

On Sunday mornings when I preach, a lot of times when I prepare the message, self tells me: "You know this is not the message for the morning," or "You know you're not ready." The devil just says a lot of things to your mind. And that's the time when I go to the pulpit, and the Lord really blesses the Word.

—Pastor and gospel singer Shirley Caesar

It must have been quite an experience growing up in the house of Philip, the zealous evangelist who first planted the Gospel in Samaria. His fervent preaching, recounted in Acts 8, triggered a powerful revival that was accompanied by healing miracles. Demons came out screaming because Philip was bold and authoritative.

After an angel directed Philip to take a desert road south toward Gaza, he met an influential Ethiopian and led him to faith. (That strategic conversion resulted in the planting of the Gospel in North Africa.) After Philip baptized the Ethiopian, he was supernaturally translated to another city, Azotus. He continued to preach all over that region and finally settled in the seaside city of Caesarea.

This guy could not stop talking about Jesus. He preached everywhere he went. So it should not surprise us that when he finally settled down long enough to find a wife and start a family, his children grew up to be prophetic preachers. In Acts 21:8–9, Luke writes:

> On the next day we left and came to Caesarea, and entering the house of Philip the evangelist, who was one of the seven, we stayed with him. Now this man had four virgin daughters who were prophetesses.

That this information about Philip's family is included in Holy Scripture is quite profound, when we consider the challenges that women faced in New Testament times. Apparently Philip, a leader in the early Church, was so eager to spread the Gospel that he did not muzzle his daughters or limit their efforts to spread the message of Christ. He believed women should be empowered to preach.

Scripture does not give us the names of Philip's four girls or where they ended up in their own missionary ventures. Considering the spiritual DNA they inherited from their famous father, it is not a stretch to imagine that they may have eventually fanned out from Israel to preach in other nations. Centuries before jet engines were invented, Philip told them how he was transported from one city to another in a miraculous fashion. He was a man on the move, and he likely imparted this missionary spirit to his daughters. I feel sure they grew up believing that God could use them to both travel and preach. They did not have to ask if girls could speak for God; their daddy believed in an equal-opportunity Gospel.

This sense of sexual equality was the prevailing ethos of the New Testament Church. When the early disciples were gathered in the Upper Room on the day of Pentecost, 120 men and women were praying together and waiting for the promised outpouring of the Holy Spirit. When the Spirit's wind began to blow, and His fire was ignited, the flames of Pentecostal power did not rest only on men's heads. No, the Bible says tongues of fire "rested on each one of them" (Acts 2:3).

In addition, when this miracle of empowerment occurred, they did not see blue flames resting on the men and pink flames on the women. The flame was the same. The power of the Spirit knows no bias. There is no "weaker female version" of the Spirit for women. The biblical account says "they were *all* filled with the Holy Spirit and began to speak with other tongues, as the Spirit was giving them utterance" (verse 4, emphasis added). When people are filled with the Spirit, whether men or women, they always speak. Boldness to speak is the primary manifestation of the Spirit's power.

After the miracle of Pentecost occurred, Peter stood to preach— and he quoted an ancient text from the prophet Joel predicting that one day women would speak courageously for God. Peter said in Acts 2:17: "'And it shall be in the last days,' God says, 'that I will pour forth of My Spirit on all mankind; and your sons and your daughters shall prophesy.'"

This is actually one of the foundational truths of the Spirit-empowered Church. Under the Old Covenant, the Jewish priesthood was limited to an elite group of males, between the ages of 25 and 50, who traced their lineage to the sons of Aaron. Yet because of the coming of Christ and the outpouring of the Spirit, the priesthood has been expanded. According to Joel's prediction, it now includes men and women from every race, age and economic and social background. Pentecost lifted restrictions and ushered in a new age of liberty in the Holy Spirit.

Where Are the Women of Fire?

Regardless of religious restrictions and poor Bible interpretations that have limited women, the Holy Spirit has empowered many women around the world to speak boldly for Him. This is especially true in the developing world. Sister Peng, a woman I met in China several years ago, has paid a high price to be a Christian. She has been arrested many times, and she will return to jail if the police catch her preaching the Gospel again. Forced to live as a fugitive, she sneaks into her home at night to visit her husband and young daughter.

The first time Peng was taken into custody, just after the Tiananmen Square massacre in Beijing in 1989, she was delivering a fresh shipment of Chinese Bibles to some unregistered pastors. She was thrown into a dirty detention cell and tortured with an electric cattle prod in an effort to force a confession of her crimes. She shivered in that cell for months. Guards offered no coat, blanket or feminine hygiene supplies.

"For eight months I had no contact with anyone. I just ate soup in my cell," Peng told me when I visited her. "It is really God's mercy that He fed me and kept me warm." When Peng was transferred to a women's prison, she spent two lonely years there. But during that time she led 32 female inmates to Christ. Upon her release, she immediately resumed her itinerant preaching ministry.

This brave woman does not let her thin frame or her femininity stop her from taking on dangerous assignments. And she is not alone. She is one of the many female heroes of China's Underground

Church movement. When I visited a group of unregistered church leaders in a city near Hong Kong, I discovered that between one-half to two-thirds of all church planters in China at that time were women. Along with their male colleagues, they were leading approximately 25,000 people to Christ daily.

One evening after a meeting with these humble Chinese leaders, I returned to my hotel room and discovered two of the female leaders waiting at my door with a translator. "They would like you to pray for them," the translator said.

"How many churches do you oversee?" I inquired. The translator pointed to the woman on the left. "This one oversees two thousand churches, and this other one oversees five thousand churches," he said. I was stunned. Some denominations in the United States are arguing about whether or not a woman can stand behind a pulpit; meanwhile, women in China are engaging in dangerous missions and governing thousands of new churches. There is something wrong with this picture!

Sister Peng is a woman with a mission. On the last day of my visit, she shared with me her plans to take teams of Chinese Christians into the Muslim republics on the western border of China, a place where she expected to encounter harsher persecution than anything she experienced under Communism. Her ultimate goal, she told me, was to see the Chinese church "march from China to Jerusalem until all the Muslim world hears the Gospel."

I wish we shared this fervor in the United States. Why do many Christian women shy away from the challenge of speaking for God? I have identified four reasons:

1. *They are too comfortable.* I know a woman named Jackie Rodriguez who is a gifted evangelist. A few years ago she took her baby with her to southern Mexico, where she preached

in several villages. She led many people to Christ during that week. Some women would balk at such a dangerous mission, but Rodriguez decided she could not excuse herself from fulfilling the Great Commission just because she was nursing a baby. She lives outside the box!

Many women—even those with young children—can be called upon by God to do exploits for His Kingdom. Of course not all women are called to preach in foreign countries. But my question is this: Are you willing to do whatever God is calling you to do? Have you taken all your objections and excuses to the cross, or are you keeping God at arm's distance because you think He might ask you to speak for Him in a way that disrupts your comfort zone?

2. *They are afraid.* God has not called any of us to live under the control of fear. Women do not have an automatic excuse to be mousy or fainthearted. In fact, the apostle Peter commanded women to renounce fear in order to be true daughters of Sarah (see 1 Peter 3:6). Have you made sure that fear is not a stumbling block in your heart?

Many people assume that having an introverted personality releases them from preaching or prophesying. They assume that God puts this calling only on extroverted people who enjoy public speaking. That is not true! Many of the people God called in the Old Testament to speak for Him felt horribly inadequate and tried to run from their callings. God typically calls the unqualified; it is usually the most reluctant who are tapped to lead.

3. *They are waiting for permission.* The conservative American church has conditioned women to be passive. For years we have told women to be quiet and to wait for men to give them instructions. Meanwhile, the Holy Spirit has been

wooing women to tune out the voice of religion so they can hear His voice.

God does not need a man's permission before He commissions a woman to do something. If you are waiting for a man's permission to commence some form of ministry, that permission may never come. You must obey the Lord's voice. When you stand before the throne of judgment, the words *My husband wouldn't let me do that* will not be a permissible excuse.

4. *They have not embraced the Great Commission.* Few American Christians, men or women, have genuine zeal to see Christ's Kingdom expand to the nations. Even though Jesus told us to seek His Kingdom first, missionary endeavors quickly drop to the bottom of our priority lists when we are distracted by materialism and the cares of this life.

But we must remember that even in this season of terrorist threats and economic instability, God has not revoked the Great Commission. He has not said to us: "That's okay. You don't have to take the Gospel to the nations right now. Wait at least until the threat of Muslim violence subsides." No, the Great Commission still stands. We must take up the challenge, swallow our fears and love not our lives "even when faced with death" (Revelation 12:11).

I believe God is calling women as never before to rise to this occasion. Every previous generation has had brave women warriors. From the days of the early Church, when women of faith were ripped to pieces by Caesar's lions, the daughters of the Church have provided a bold witness. Where are these women of fire? My prayer is that they will emerge in this decade with hotter zeal, deeper compassion and stronger commitment than at any other time in history.

Step Up to the Microphone

Even though I speak often in churches and at conferences, I have found that preaching the Gospel is one of the most challenging assignments anyone could possibly volunteer for. After one particularly discouraging experience in which an audience stared coldly at me, arms folded, I faced the fact that preaching is not my calling. I shared my struggle with an older pastor.

"Sometimes I feel really discouraged after I speak," I told my friend. "Does that ever happen to you?" I was sure he would confirm that preaching was not my spiritual gift. His answer shocked me.

"Son," he said, "I have felt like that every Monday morning since I've been in the ministry."

When I tell my friends that I have never felt gifted for public speaking, and that I stubbornly resisted the call of God on my life because of my lack of confidence, they act surprised. Most of us assume that people who are involved in public preaching want to be there. Think again!

The power of prophetic preaching actually works the opposite of the way we think it should. If we view things carnally, we assume that God chooses gifted orators who then hone and shape their skills—like a doctor who learns surgery or an actor who learns to perform on stage. But true prophetic preaching is not a natural exercise—it is actually one of the most supernatural tasks anyone can ever be called to do. It requires an imperfect human vessel to yield himself or herself in order to speak the very words of God.

No wonder most of the leaders we encounter in the Bible were reluctant! Moses made excuses about being slow of speech, Gideon tried to disqualify himself, and Jeremiah complained to the Lord about the weighty responsibility of carrying a prophetic burden. Jonah bought a one-way ticket to the other side of the Mediterranean Sea so he would not have to give his unpopular sermon.

And the apostle Paul, who was a silver-tongued Pharisee before he met Christ, was stripped of his worldly eloquence before he preached throughout the Roman Empire. He told the Corinthians:

> I was with you in weakness and in fear and in much trembling, and my message and my preaching were not in persuasive words of wisdom, but in demonstration of the Spirit and of power, so that your faith would not rest on the wisdom of men, but on the power of God.
>
> 1 Corinthians 2:3–5

Revivalist Arthur Katz wrote about the power of true preaching in his 1999 book *Apostolic Foundations*:

> The only one qualified to preach . . . is the one who wants to run the other way, like Jonah. The man, however, who loves to talk, loves to be public, and enjoys being seen and heard, need not think that a word like this will ever be emitted from his mouth. The man who sighs and groans when called upon to speak, who does not want to be there, who feels terribly uncomfortable, who knows that he is not going to be understood, is the man out of whose mouth the word of true preaching is most likely to come.[1]

If we try to preach or prophesy—or pursue any walk such as those we have studied—in the flesh, the results will be miserable; but if we wholly trust the power of the Spirit, our obedience will unleash God to move through us however He desires.

No one will say that this is easy. Fears and doubts are going to assail us regularly. But remember: The Kingdom is not built on self-confidence. We need daughters who will speak God's words—as well as pioneer new trails, mentor young people, worship, fight, forsake the past and innumerable other ministries and callings. The Kingdom will not move forward until broken, reluctant, weak and trembling men and women allow His holy fire to fill them.

Don't be intimidated by the challenge. God wants to use your mouth, just as He put a holy fire into the mouths of Philip's daughters in the first century. You can speak for God, and when you do His message will flow out of you.

It is time to bury all of those "I'm just a woman" excuses. I challenge you to break from tradition, pursue the Holy Spirit's boldness and allow God's call on your life to become like a fire in your bones. You will never be the same. And you will never regret it.

─────── LET'S TALK ABOUT IT ───────

1. Why is it significant that the New Testament evangelist named Philip had four daughters who were prophetesses?
2. On the day of Pentecost, Peter declared that when the Holy Spirit was poured out on the Church, "your sons and daughters will prophesy." What does this mean for women today?
3. Share honestly how you feel about speaking for God. Are you shy? Do you feel reluctant to share your faith, give a testimony or speak to others about God?
4. What barriers might be keeping you from being able to speak for God boldly? Are you willing to overcome these barriers?

─────── A MESSAGE FROM YOUR HEAVENLY FATHER ───────

My precious daughter,

Regardless of the fears you have struggled with in the past, I can set you free to speak for Me. I am your liberator. Don't be afraid of people, and don't care what they say or think about you. I have called you to be a bold witness. When I want you to speak for Me, I will give you the right words, the precise timing and the courage to deliver My message. Don't shrink back in timidity. I have not given you a spirit of fear, but I have given you power and love and discipline. Let Me fill you with the power of the Holy Spirit. As you receive My power, new boldness will rise in your heart and you will discover new grace to speak. Don't use your womanhood as an excuse to shrink back. Just as I made Philip's daughters into mighty prophetesses, I will make you My prophetic messenger.

Appendix

How to Begin Your Journey with God

The fearless daughters of the Bible that we have studied in this book all have this in common: They began or grew in relationship with God. By overcoming fears and prejudices, they challenged tradition, fought injustice and dared to lead. Do you, like them, stand before God, ready to do His will?

Being in right relationship with God begins by knowing that your sins can be forgiven through Jesus' atoning death on the cross. If you have never made the decision to commit your life to Jesus, here are five simple steps you can take to begin a relationship with Him that will last through eternity. A prayer is provided at the end of these steps to help guide you as you speak to Him.

1. *Recognize your need.* The Bible tells us that "all have sinned and fall short of the glory of God" (Romans 3:23). All of us are sinners, and we must admit our need for a Savior.

2. *Repent of your sins.* Because God is completely holy, our sins create a wall that separates us from Him. By confessing your sins you will find forgiveness. "Repent" means to make a 180-degree turnaround. The Bible promises: "If we confess our sins, He is faithful and righteous to forgive us our sins and to cleanse us from all unrighteousness" (1 John 1:9).

3. *Believe in Jesus.* God worked a miracle when He sent His only Son to die for us. We do not have to pay the penalty for our sins: Jesus paid it all! We cannot work for our salvation. It is a gift from God, and all He requires is that we believe. Put your faith in Him. The Bible says: "For God so loved the world, that He gave His only begotten Son, that whoever believes in Him shall not perish, but have eternal life" (John 3:16).

4. *Receive His salvation.* God has given us this free gift, but we must accept it. Thank Him for sending Jesus to die on the cross for you. Thank Him for His amazing love, mercy and forgiveness. Then ask Him to live in your heart. His promise to us is sure: "But as many as received Him, to them He gave the right to become children of God" (John 1:12).

5. *Confess your faith.* The Bible assures us: "If you confess with your mouth Jesus as Lord, and believe in your heart that God raised Him from the dead, you will be saved" (Romans 10:9). You have been born again and are now part of God's family. Tell someone else what Jesus has done in your life! This amazing experience can be yours. Embrace God's love and receive the salvation that only Jesus Christ gives.

Pray this prayer:

Lord, thank You for sending Your only Son, Jesus Christ, to die for me. I have been separated from You, but I choose to turn away from all my sins today. Forgive me for trying to live apart from You. I believe You are the one and only true God, and I want to know You intimately. Thank You that because of Jesus' death on the cross, I have been forgiven. I ask You to wash me completely clean of all my sins, and restore me to fellowship with You. I invite Jesus to come into my heart and cause me to be born again. I believe He is the Son of God. Amen.

Notes

Chapter 1: Sarah, the Mother of Our Faith

1. "Medieval Women," *History Learning Site*, accessed March 29, 2012, http://www.historylearningsite.co.uk/medieval_women.htm.

2. "Margaret Heffernan Borland," *Great Texas Women (The University of Texas at Austin)*, accessed March 29, 2012, http://www.utexas.edu/gtw/borland.php.

3. Jeanie Rose, "Faith-filled Abraham," *Pray the Scriptures*, accessed March 29, 2012, http://www.pray-the-scriptures.com/faithbelieve/faithofabraham/abraham.html.

4. For a full explanation of the word *ezer* and its meaning, see J. Lee Grady, *10 Lies the Church Tells Women* (Lake Mary, Fla.: Charisma House, 2000), 33–35.

Chapter 2: The Five Daughters of Zelophehad

1. "Rosa Parks," *Famous Women IMHO*, accessed March 29, 2012, http://www.famouswomenimho.com/rosa-parks.htm.

2. "Rosa Parks and the Montgomery Bus Boycott," *The Black History Wall*, accessed March 29, 2012, http://blackhistorywall.wordpress.com/2010/02/04/february-4-rosa-parks-and-the-montgomery-bus-boycott-2/.

3. Anne Adams, "Rosa Parks: The Lady Said 'No,'" *History's Women: The Unsung Heroines*, accessed March 29, 2012, http://www.historyswomen.com/socialreformer/rosaparks2.html.

4. Gary Younge, "Taking a Stand by Sitting Down," *The Guardian*, October 26, 2005, http://www.guardian.co.uk/world/2005/oct/26/usa.garyyounge.

5. Jennifer Kim, "Tired of Giving In: Remembering Rosa Parks," *The Ella Baker Center for Human Rights*, October 22, 2010, http://ellabaker center.org/blog/2010/10/tired-of-giving-in-remembering-rosa-parks.

6. "Condoleezza Rice," *Wikipedia*, last modified March 28, 2012, http:// en.wikipedia.org/wiki/Condoleezza_Rice.

7. Ibid.

Chapter 3: Ruth, the Moabite

1. The confidential interview with "Sheryl" was conducted by the author in February 2012. Her real name is withheld to protect her identity.

2. "National Statistics," *Domestic Violence Resource Center*, accessed March 29, 2012, http://www.dvrc-or.org/domestic/violence/resources/C61/.

3. "Intimate Partner Violence: Myths vs. Facts," *The University of Southern California Rossier School of Education*, accessed March 29, 2012, http:// rsoeweb2.usc.edu:8080/sv/ipv2.html.

Chapter 4: Achsah, Daughter of Caleb

1. Howard Butt Jr., "The Lady from Possum Trot and Why Her Barn Had Spires," *Christianity Today*, accessed March 29, 2012, http://www.christianity today.com/workplace/articles/ourhighcalling/ladypossumtrot.html.

2. "Martha Berry," *About North Georgia*, accessed March 29, 2012, http:// ngeorgia.com/ang/Martha_Berry.

3. Sagarika Satapathy, "Mother Teresa: The Global Icon of Selfless Social Service," *The Social Work for Mankind* (blog), February 25, 2011, http://www .indiansocialstudy.com/2011/02/mother-teresa-quotations-and-favorite.html.

Chapter 5: Hannah, Mother of Samuel

1. "Amy Carmichael, God's Missionary," *The Elisabeth Elliot Newsletter*, May/June 2002, http://www.elisabethelliot.org/newsletters/2002-05-06.pdf.

Chapter 6: Esther, Queen of Persia

1. "About Mary," *The Mary Slessor Foundation*, accessed March 29, 2012, http://maryslessor.org/mary-slessor.

2. Eugene Myers Harrison, "Mary Slessor: The White Queen of Calabar," *Wholesome Words*, accessed March 29, 2012, http://www.wholesomewords .org/missions/bioslessor2.html.

3. Nicole Partridge, "One Woman and a Great Big God," *Charisma*, 2009, 42.

4. "Missing Women," *WikiGender*, last modified February 16, 2012, http:// www.wikigender.org/index.php/Missing_Women.

5. "Human Trafficking: The Facts," *UN Global Initiative to Fight Human Trafficking*, accessed March 29, 2012, http://www.unglobalcompact

.org/docs/issues_doc/labour/Forced_labour/HUMAN_TRAFFICKING_-_
THE_FACTS_-_final.pdf.

6. C. S. Lewis, *The Screwtape Letters* (New York: HarperCollins, 1942), 68.

7. William Pringle Livingstone, *Mary Slessor of Calabar* (London: Hodder and Stoughton, 1916), 295.

Chapter 7: Miriam, Sister of Moses

1. Quotes from Pastor Indri Gautama are from an interview conducted by the author in Jakarta, Indonesia, in 2008.

2. For an extensive discussion of the Greek word *authentein*, and the background of 1 Timothy 2:12, see Richard Clark Kroeger and Catherine Clark Kroeger, *I Suffer Not a Woman* (Grand Rapids: Baker, 1992). See especially chapters 7 and 8.

3. Catherine Mumford Booth, "Female Ministry; or, Woman's Right to Preach the Gospel," *The Voice* (*Christian Resource Institute*), accessed March 29, 2012, http://www.crivoice.org/WT-cbooth.html.

4. Charles Spurgeon, "New Uses for Old Trophies," *Bible Bulletin Board*, accessed March 29, 2012, http://www.biblebb.com/files/spurgeon/0972.htm.

Chapter 8: Deborah, Judge of Israel

1. Quotes from Natalia Schedrivaya are from an interview conducted by the author in Kiev, Ukraine, in February 2006.

Chapter 9: Jehosheba, Daughter of King Joram

1. Stephen C. Gammie and Randy J. Nelson, "Maternal Aggression Is Reduced in Neutronal Nitric Oxide Synthase Deficient Mice," *Journal of Neuroscience* 19:18 (September 15, 1999), 8027–8035.

2. Ibid.

3. Corrie ten Boom, *The Hiding Place* (Grand Rapids: Chosen, 1971), 47.

Chapter 10: Mary, the Mother of Jesus

1. R. T. Kendall, "The Case for the Virgin Birth," *Charisma*, December 2009, 53.

2. Stephen Ross, "Missionary Quotes," *Wholesome Words*, accessed March 29, 2012, http://www.wholesomewords.org/missions/msquotes.html.

Chapter 11: Mary of Bethany

1. "Papers of Fanny Crosby," *Billy Graham Center Archives*, last revised October 23, 2000, http://www2.wheaton.edu/bgc/archives/GUIDES/035.htm#3.

2. Fanny Crosby, *Fanny Crosby: An Autobiography* (Peabody, Mass.: Hendrickson, 2008), 127.

3. "Fanny Crosby," *Wikipedia*, last modified March 28, 2012, http://en.wikipedia.org/wiki/Fanny_Crosby.

4. Ibid.

5. Kenneth W. Osbeck, *101 More Hymn Stories* (Grand Rapids: Kregel, 1985), 239–40.

6. J. M. K., "Safe in the Arms of Jesus," *Wholesome Words*, accessed March 29, 2012, http://www.wholesomewords.org/biography/bcrosby3.html.

7. "Fanny Crosby: America's Hymn Queen," *Christianity.com*, accessed March 29, 2012, http://www.christianity.com/ChurchHistory/11630385/.

8. "Spikenard," *Wikipedia*, last modified March 25, 2012, http://en.wikipedia.org/wiki/Spikenard.

9. Shawn Rose, "Mary's Alabaster Box," *SermonCentral.com*, accessed March 29, 2012, http://www.sermoncentral.com/sermons/marys-alabaster-box-shawn-rose-sermon-on-giving-yourself-152160.asp.

Chapter 12: The Samaritan Woman

1. Beatrice Lamwaka, "Ugandans Urge Change in Attitudes Toward Domestic Violence," *Global Press Institute*, accessed March 29, 2012, http://www.globalpressinstitute.org/global-news/africa/uganda/ugandans-urge-change-attitudes-toward-domestic-violence.

2. Ken Walker, "The Preacher Who Tells It Like It Is," *Charisma*, November 1998, 50.

3. Ibid., 53.

Chapter 14: Priscilla, Spiritual Daughter of the Apostle Paul

1. Billy Graham, foreword to *The Henrietta Mears Story*, by Barbara Hudson Powers (Old Tappan, N.J.: Revell, 1957), 7.

2. Wendy Murray Zoba, "The Grandmother of Us All," *Christianity Today*, September 16, 1996, http://www.christianitytoday.com/ct/1996/september16/6ta044.html.

3. James Kiefer, "Aquila and Priscilla: Companions of the Apostle Paul," *Biographical Sketches of Memorable Christians of the Past*, accessed March 29, 2012, http://justus.anglican.org/resources/bio/41.html.

4. For a detailed study of the theory that Priscilla wrote the book of Hebrews, see Ruth Hoppin, *Priscilla's Letter: Finding the Author of the Epistle to the Hebrews* (Fort Bragg, Calif.: Lost Coast Press, 1997).

Chapter 15: The Four Daughters of Philip the Evangelist

1. Arthur Katz, *Apostolic Foundations*, (Burning Bush Publications, 1999).

Index

Index

J. Lee Grady began his ministry career as a Christian journalist. A native of Atlanta, Georgia, and graduate of Berry College, he served as editor of a campus ministry publication for several years before joining the staff of *Charisma* magazine in 1992. He worked there for eighteen years, and for eleven of those years served as editor. During that time he launched The Mordecai Project, a ministry focused on empowering women leaders and confronting the abuse of women globally.

Since 2010 Lee has worked with The Mordecai Project full-time. Now an ordained minister, he has conducted conferences and seminars in 26 countries. In 2011 he began building a network of compassion projects in nations where women and girls suffer most from abuse, abandonment and discrimination. He opened his first girls' home in India in 2011, and is planning to establish more girls' homes as well as shelters for abused women in Uganda, Peru, Guatemala, Nigeria, Ecuador and other nations.

Lee is the author of four other books: *10 Lies the Church Tells Women* (Charisma House, 2000), *25 Tough Questions About Women and the Church* (Charisma House, 2003), *The Holy Spirit Is Not for Sale* (Chosen, 2010) and *10 Lies Men Believe* (Charisma House, 2011). He writes a weekly column for *Charisma* called "Fire in My Bones" (www.fireinmybones.com), in which he challenges Christians to pursue the genuine power of the Holy Spirit.

Lee and his wife, Deborah, live in the Orlando, Florida, area. They have been married for 28 years, and they have four grown daughters. You can learn more about The Mordecai Project at: www.themordecaiproject.org. You can write Lee at:

The Mordecai Project
c/o Christian Life Missions
PO Box 952248
Lake Mary, Florida 32795

More Insights on Spiritual Leadership From J. Lee Grady

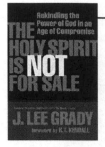

With his finger on the pulse of the Spirit-filled movements, J. Lee Grady has recently observed some distressing trends. In this book he exposes the problems and scandals that plague today's churches and ministries—including abuse, showmanship, manipulation and infatuation with prosperity. Yet his message isn't one of condemnation, but rather, it's a call to action. It's time for Christians to return to their biblical roots and restore boldness, integrity and humility for true spiritual renewal.

The Holy Spirit Is Not for Sale

chosenbooks.com

43825433R00148

Made in the USA
Lexington, KY
14 August 2015